GENUINE MEMOIRS
OF
ASIATICUS

GENUINE MEMOIRS

OF

ASIATICUS:

IN A SERIES OF

LETTERS TO A FRIEND,

DURING FIVE YEARS RESIDENCE IN
DIFFERENT PARTS OF INDIA

PHILIP DORMER STANHOPE

GYAN

Published by

Gyan Publishing House
5, Ansari Road
Daryaganj, New Delhi-110002
Phone: 011-47034999, 9811692060
E-mail: books@gyanbooks.com

Distribution Network
gyanbooks.com
India, USA, Canada, UK, Australia

ISBN: 978-93-7133-702-1 (PB)

First Published, 1784

2nd Impression 2025

Printed at: Gyan Press, Delhi.

GENUINE MEMOIRS OF ASIATICUS
Author: PHILIP DORMER STANHOPE

GENUINE MEMOIRS

OF

ASIATICUS,

IN A SERIES OF

LETTERS to a FRIEND,

DURING FIVE YEARS RESIDENCE IN DIFFERENT PARTS OF INDIA, THREE OF WHICH WERE SPENT IN THE SERVICE OF THE

NABOB of ARCOT.

INTERSPERSED WITH

ANECDOTES OF SEVERAL WELL-KNOWN

CHARACTERS,

AND CONTAINING AN IMPARTIAL ACCOUNT OF THE CONFINEMENT AND

DEATH of LORD PIGOT,

AND OF

The Share the NABOB of ARCOT had in that *MEMORABLE TRANSACTION.*

By PHILIP DORMER STANHOPE, Esq.
Late of the First Regiment of Dragoon Guards.

LONDON.
Printed for G. KEARSLEY, at No. 46, Fleet Street.
MDCCLXXXIV.
Entered at Stationers Hall.

TO THE

Hon. WARREN HASTINGS,

Governor General of India.

S I R,

I Have preſumed to dedicate the following ſheets to you, as the only tribute of gratitude in my power to lay at your feet in return for that protection, with which you condeſcended to honour me in Bengal. To do impartial juſtice to your ſhining abilities and known integrity of heart is beyond my feeble efforts. To ſay, that through your ſpirited exertions the affairs of the Honourable Company have been retrieved from ruin, and the bleſſings of peace in great meaſure reſtored throughout the Eaſtern world, falls infinitely ſhort of that praiſe which

is

is due to your exalted character. That you may long remain in that high station, which you have filled with so much honour to yourself and advantage to your country, is the sincere wish of every true friend to the British empire, and of,

SIR,

Your most devoted,

Obliged,

And obedient servant,

Philip Dormer Stanhope.

Feb. 1784.

MEMOIRS

OF

ASIATICUS.

LETTER I.

Euphrates, Indiaman, in the Downs,
December, 1773.

My Dear Friend,

I Embrace the firſt moment which the confuſion of the new ſcene before me, and the unſettled ſtate of my own mind will allow, to comunicate to you the pleaſing intelligence of my eſcape from the dangers which threatened me, and which I had every reaſon to fear would effectually deſtroy all my golden dreams of Eaſtern magnificence. You are well acquainted with the unfortunate connexion which

 occaſioned

occaſioned my ſudden departure from the Univerſity, and you know that my creditors, enraged to ſee every proſpect of payment in one moment loſt by that imprudent ſtep, omitted no means which their ingenuity could point out, to diſcover the place of my retreat. I now moſt ſincerely wiſh that retreat had been rendered leſs agreeable to me, or that the amiable Charlotte had been leſs ſuſceptible of thoſe tender impreſſions, which though highly flattering to my vanity, yet I confeſs to you my heart ſecretly diſapproved. I was not yet ſo enamoured with ruin, as to think of matrimony, and I knew that no greater torment could be inflicted on a ſoft believing females than the pangs of diſappointed love. You have formerly ſeen Miſs Rivers, and you have called her handſome, and you may believe me, when I aſſure you that ſhe poſſeſſes every virtue that can adorn the female mind. But that uncommon ſenſibility, and thoſe romantic ideas, ſo inſeparably connected with

with a country education, muſt ever prove to her a ſource of unhappineſs, and muſt render even the moſt innocent pleaſures highly dangerous in their conſequences.

When the hoſpitality of Mr. Rivers had in ſome degree removed the unfavourable ideas I had entertained of a country life, I began to promiſe myſelf an infinite fund of amuſement in the converſation of his amiable daughter. Her natural good humour led her to omit no opportunity of making the hours paſs agreeably away, and of diſpelling that melancholly which I in vain endeavoured to conceal. We walked together in the garden, upon the ſea-beach, and in the neighbouring woods; while her mother devoted her time to her domeſtic concerns, and my worthy friend, engaged among his labourers in the field, little thought that I ſhould repay his kindneſs by ſeducing the affections of his daughter, and diſturbing the peace of a family, whoſe hoſpitable roof had received me, when, like Adam expelled from

Paradiſe, I had the whole world before me and providence my guide.

However, to cut ſhort a ſcene which at this moment fills me with grief and confuſion, I will only ſay, that in an unlucky moment I made her a propoſal of marriage, and that our hours imperceptibly glided away in the enjoyment of thoſe pleaſures which only lovers know, till a ſummons from my father to attend him in London previous to my embarkation for India at once diſſolved all our aerial ſchemes of future happineſs, and plunged the whole family into inexpreſſible diſtreſs. You, who have been no ſtranger to ſcenes like this, and who well know by what miſtaken principles even men of ſenſe are led aſtray, when paſſion has drowned the voice of reaſon, can eaſily picture to yourſelf the reproaches of the weeping mother, and the rage of the father denouncing immediate vengeance, and calling aloud for ſatisfaction from the ungrateful ſerpent, whom he had foſtered ed in his boſom, and even treated with parental tenderneſs. Such, my friend, would have been the behaviour of thoſe fathers, to whom the misjudging world too often aſcribes the merit of ſuperior wiſdom, and who, while they hold happineſs to be inſeparable from wealth, are ready to beſtow every bleſſing upon their children but real felicity. Mr. Rivers however acted a very different part; he neither reproached me with ingratitude, nor did he expreſs any concern, except for the impoſſibility of that union, which he was obliging enough to ſay, under other circumſtances, would have given him the greateſt pleaſure. He aſſured me, that he ſhould ever conſider my intereſt as immediately connected with his own; and even conſented that Miſs Rivers ſhould wait until my return from India; when he hoped, that every obſtacle that now impeded our happineſs would be removed. You may ſuppoſe, that I felt myſelf highly pleaſed at this unexpected declaration, and that I omitted nothing in my reply which could convince him of the ſincerity of my intentions, whenever fortune ſhould enable me to fulfil my engagements. Indeed he ſeemed perfectly ſatisfied with me, and ſaid every thing which friendſhip could ſuggeſt to inſpire me with fortitude to go through the affecting ſcene which now preſented itſelf. The day was at hand which was to ſeparate me, perhaps for ever, from my beloved Charlotte. My feelings on this occaſion I ſhall not attempt to deſcribe. Imagine to yourſelf, that I left the houſe of my friend overwhelmed with grief, and that all the pomp and pride of Aſiatic grandeur had in that moment no charms for me.

I am, &c.

LETTER II.

Madeira, Feb. 1774.

AFTER a tedious paſſage of two and thirty days, I feel myſelf extremely happy in being once more permitted to ſet my foot upon dry land, and to breathe the freſh air among a race of beings, who, though not the moſt cultivated I ever met with, are yet infinitely ſuperior to thoſe unmannerly Hottentots, who call themſelves the officers of the ſhip, which it has been my misfortune to chuſe as the vehicle of my tranſportation from my native country. Indeed before I had been many minutes on board, I formed a moſt unfavourable idea of my ſituation from an object which preſented itſelf to my view; and which, though I ſuppoſe perfectly familiar to the petty tyrants of the ocean, appeared to me utterly inconſiſtent with the laws and cuſtoms

of

of a civilized nation. One of those unfortunate creatures, whom the agents of the East India company, by ſpecious advertiſements, and by various ſtratagems calculated to deceive the ignorant and the unwary, have entrapped into their ſervice, had by ſome act of diſreſpect incurred the diſpleaſure of the chief mate, or officer, in whom (under the controul of the captain) the executive power is chiefly lodged. This miſerable wretch, though evidently in a ſtate of delirium, the conſequence of that intoxication which had been made the inſtrument of his captivity, was, by order of the great man, immediately loaded with irons; an immenſe gag faſtened in his mouth; and for the further crime of expreſſing his diſſatisfaction at this inhuman uſage he was beaten over the head and face with a large cane, till he ſunk down ſenſeleſs upon the deck, and the tyrant began to tremble, leaſt the conſequences of his barbarity ſhould in the end prove fatal to himſelf,

himſelf. I ventured to hint to one of my fellow paſſengers my abhorrence of ſuch cruelty, and was told that if I ſuffered a ſingle word to eſcape my lips, which might convey the ſlighteſt offence to any one of thoſe *gentlemen* under whoſe abſolute command I was, I ſhould certainly meet with every inſult that could render my ſituation uncomfortable, and ſhould perhaps be confined the reſt of the voyage to my cabbin, under pretence of having conduced to leſſen the authority of the captain, and ſow a ſpirit of diſſention and mutiny among the crew.

However I will quit ſo diſagreeable a ſubject, and proceed to give you ſome account of the iſland of Madeira, which after a months confinement in my floating priſon, ſeems to me quite a terreſtrial Paradiſe. Madeira, which is the largeſt of the Canary iſlands, is ſituate in the Atlantic ocean, in ſixteen degrees of W. L. and thirty-three of N. L. and is about one hundred

miles

miles in circumference. The climate, though perhaps the finest in the world, must certainly be deemed hot by an inhabitant of the more northern latitudes. When first discovered by the Portuguese in the beginning of the fifteenth century, it was entirely covered with wood, which being consumed by fire, the ashes have so fertilized the soil, that it produces incredible quantities of wine, which has this peculiar quality, that it keeps best in the hottest climates, and therefore scarce any other is drank either in the East or West Indies. The principal town, which is called Fonchal, is ill built and ugly, the streets are narrow, and the houses inconvenient. The churches and convents are very numerous, and the nuns, at least all those who are exposed to public view, have such very little pretensions to personal charms, that their vows of chastity seem rather to have been the effect of necessity than of choice. They supply themselves with pocket-money by the sale of sword knots,

cockades,

cockades, and other trumpery, which they convey through the double grates by means of a cleft ſtick to their Engliſh viſitors. The inquiſition flouriſhes here in all its horrors, and the lower orders of people pay almoſt divine honours to the prieſts. The town is garriſoned by a few companies of ſoldiers, whoſe appearance is totally unmartial, and who I believe would diſplay very little military heroiſm in the ſervice of his moſt faithful majeſty, ſhould an enemy invade Madeira. The harbour is defended by a ſmall fort erected on the ſummit of a rock about three hundred yards diſtant from the main iſland, and acceſſable only by a winding and exceedingly narrow flight of ſteps. The Portugueſe repoſe great confidence in this place of ſtrength, and think it impregnable; but in my opinion a ſingle frigate would ſoon ſilence its batteries, and lay the town in aſhes. The principal tavern, in which I have taken up my reſidence, is a large houſe ill contrived and ſhabbily furniſhed.

furnished. It is kept by an Irishman who has a pretty wife, of whom he is extremely jealous. I live at the expence of near a guinea each day, for which I have a bad dinner and execrable wine, and I amuse myself in the evening at backgammon with a priest, who is at least eighty years of age, above sixty of which he has spent upon the island.

Tomorrow I expect to return on board, for at least ten weeks to be fatigued with the same dull unvaried prospect of sky and water, and to be immured with savages, whose manners are as unpolished, as if they had been educated in the wildest deserts of Siberia. With what regret do I now look back on those happy hours which I spent with my lovely Charlotte, whose image is ever present to my imagination in all the charms of native innocence and blooming youth.

My fellow passengers, whom I suppose a similarity of circumstances has collected from every quarter of the world, and engaged

gaged in the ſame purſuit after the riches of the Eaſt, form a group altogether entertaining enough, was my heart ſufficiently at eaſe to be amuſed with trifles. They conſiſt of two young ladies, who go out under the immediate protection of the Captain, in hopes that ſome wealthy Nabob may be attracted by the power of thoſe charms, which they had in vain diſplayed at Highgate aſſembly, and at the city balls; an elderly gentleman who formerly amaſſed a conſiderable fortune by trade in India, which he loſt by ſpeculaing in the Engliſh funds; a young Hibernian, who finds it neceſſary to travel, till time ſhall have cooled the reſentment of ſeveral noble families, whoſe ſons and heirs have fallen by his hand in duels; and a captain of the Bengal artillery, who reviſited England in conſequence of a wound he received in a rencounter with a tyger, and who daily amuſes us with the various feats by which he has ſignalized himſelf, in the deſtruction of hyænas, and wild buffalos. This motly group, with your humble ſervant, occupy the great cabbin, the ladies in a ſeparate apartment, and the gentlemen actually ſtowed on ſhelves juſt big enough to receive a ſmall mattreſs, like bales of cloth in a linen-draper's ſhop. I aſſure you, no love-ſick damſel ever longed for her wedding day with more eagerneſs, than I look forward to that happy hour, when I ſhall be landed on the Indian ſhore.

LETTER III.

Cape of Good Hope, May, 1774.

I HAVE now the ſatisfaction of acquainting my friend, that after a paſſage ſufficiently tedious and unpleaſant, I once more experience the comforts of life in the houſe of a fat, honeſt, and hoſpitable Dutchman. I will not trouble you with the occurrences of a voyage, in which, I ſuppoſe, we met with the uſual accidents that attend on contrary winds, and ſtormy weather.

Imagine to yourſelf, that for ſeveral days ſucceſſively, the waves roſe mountains high, the winds roared the ſailors vied with the elements in noiſe, and that I betook myſelf quietly to my ſhelf, where I meditated on paſt follies, and formed aerial ſchemes of future wealth and magnificence. My companions indeed ſeemed to think that theſe inconveniencies were

 amply

amply compenſated by the pleaſure of feaſting daily on turtle, of which we catched no leſs than ſixty of an enormous ſize at the iſland of Aſcenſion, where theſe animals are in amazing plenty, and are ſo much eſteemed for the ſuperior flavour of their fat, that I wonder thoſe ſons of gluttony, the aldermen of London, have not eſtabliſhed a turtle-fiſhery upon the ſpot.

Aſcenſion is a ſmall uninhabited iſland, midway between the coaſt of Africa and the Brazils. The beach is covered with innumerable ſea-birds, which depoſit their eggs in the ſand, and are ſo exceedingly tame, that they will ſuffer you to tread on them as you walk along. In the centre of the iſland is a valley thinly covered with graſs, where a few ſcattered buſhes afford ſhelter to ſome goats formerly left there by an Indiaman; and there is a ſpring of water, but not large enough to be of any uſe to the ſhips, which touch here upon their return from India for the

ſole

ſole purpoſe of catching turtle. It is very unuſual for an outward-bound ſhip to call here, and what induced our captain in ſo wanton a manner to loſe his time is, I believe, known only to himſelf. The mode of catching theſe animals is curious, and great activity is neceſſary in the undertaking. During the moon-light nights the female turtle come on ſhore to lay their eggs, and to ſleep upon the ſand. The ſailors, who go on ſhore early in the evening, poſt themſelves at a conſiderable diſtance, obſerving the moſt profound ſilence, as the ſmalleſt noiſe would inſtantly alarm the turtle, and occaſion their precipitate retreat into the water. At a proper opportunity they ſteal ſoftly towards their prey, and the unfortunate unreſiſting turtle are thrown upon their backs, and left in that poſition till the morning, when they are conveyed to the ſhip, and are laid in rows upon the deck. Upwards of five hundred eggs have ſometimes been found in one turtle; and it is remarkable, though they waſte conſiderably, yet they will live ſeveral weeks without the leaſt nouriſhment, and require only to be refreſhed morning and evening with water.

I here cannot forbear mentioning a circumſtance, which ſhocking as it is to humanity, yet perfectly correſponded with the ideas I had before entertained of the brutality of an Engliſh ſailor. Our men confeſſed that they had turned upwards of forty turtle more than they had brought on board, which they had left to periſh by inches upon the beach, merely becauſe they would not ſubmit to the trouble of replacing them in a poſture to help themſelves. Strange that ſuch barbarity ſhould be familiar to the heart of man, and above all others of thoſe men, whoſe ſituation, replete with danger, and hourly teeming with death and deſtruction, ought to inſpire them with ſentiments of univerſal benevolence, and teach them to pity even a

poor

poor helpleſs turtle expiring upon a deſert ſhore.

The Cape of Good Hope is the moſt ſouthern promontary of Africa, ſituate in ſixteen degrees of E. L. and about thirty-four of S. L. The climate is hot, but ſo extremely healthy, that the gentlemen who reſide in India, when enervated by the diſorders incident to the country, and by their own debaucheries, ſeldom fail to re-eſtabliſh their healths by a ſhort viſit to the Cape. The fruits of the earth are produced here in the greateſt perfection; and veniſon, fiſh, and poultry are in ſuch abundance, that under an Engliſh government I know no place where a perſon of moderate income might live more comfortably. You may eaſily judge how cheap all the articles of life muſt be, when I aſſure you that I pay the trifling ſum of one dollar each day for my board and lodging, and that my dinner, including an elegant deſſert and a moſt plentiful allowance of the *vin du païs* would not diſgrace difgrace the table of an Englifh gentleman of three thoufand a year eftate. The Company's gardens, which are the place of fashionable refort, are as large as St. James's park; the walks are kept in excellent order, and are fhaded by beautiful rows of Englifh oak. The governor's houfe, which is a large handfome building, ftands in the centre, and is after the prevailing fafhion of the Dutch almoft furrounded by a canal, and at the upper end is a collection of the various wild beafts, which the uncultivated forefts of Africa produce.

At prefent the converfation of the town is entirely taken up with the duel lately fought between the celebrated Captain David Roche, generally known by the appellation of Tyger Roche, and Captain Fergufon belonging to the Company's land forces in Bengal. Fergufon fell in the engagement, and the ftory is here told rather to the difadvantage of Roche; but I believe there were no witneffes, who could prove

prove the leaſt improper behaviour on the part of Roche, and that his accuſers were influenced by a moſt unjuſt and cruel prejudice. However, he ſecured his retreat on board a French ſhip then lying in the harbour, and is by this time arrived in India; the ſeverity of the Dutch laws againſt duelling rendering it abſolutely neceſſary for him to adopt the moſt expeditious mode of eſcaping from their territories.

Our ſtay at this agreeable place will not exceed ten days, when we ſhall bid farewell to the ſight of land till we arrive on the Coromandel coaſt.

LETTER. IV.

Joanna, July, 1774.

WHEN we left the Cape, I little thought any occurrence would have happened previous to our arrival in India worthy the notice of my friend; but I find myself agreeably disappointed by the sudden resolution of the captain to touch at the island of Joanna, where we arrived the twenty-ninth of June, and found two East Indiamen, one of which will sail to-morrow for England, and the other lies dismasted and deserted by her crew upon a reef of rocks, which project about a mile into the sea, near the entrance of the harbour for which they were steering with a fair wind and under an easy sail, when the neglect or ignorance of the officer on duty occasioned this melancholly event. On board this ship the unfortunate Roche had

taken

taken his paſſage at the iſland of Bourbon to proſecute his voyage to Bombay, when his evil deſtiny threw him into his preſent deplorable ſituation. He now leads a moſt unhappy life amidſt the execrations of the ſeamen who look on him as another Jonas, and think themſelves involved in the puniſhment, which the Almighty thus miraculouſly has inflicted upon the wretch who has dared to violate his commandments.

Whatever the faults of Roche may be, I am ſure the want of hoſpitality is not one. Having formerly known his ſiſter, who is married to one of the judges lately appointed to Bengal, I took the liberty of introducing myſelf, and was received by him in his Indian hut with a politeneſs and affability which would have done honour to a more ſplendid manſion. I was ſhocked to ſee a gentleman, who had once experienced all the elegancies of life, labouring under ſuch unmerited diſtreſs, and was eaſily perſuaded to alleviate the horrors

horrors of his ſolitude, during the few days we ſhall remain at Joanna, by bringing my bed on ſhore, and ſharing with him the conveniencies of his hut, which though not overburthened with furniture or with ſuperfluous ornaments, is yet a very comfortable retreat, when compared to a dirty cabbin. He related to me all the circumſtances of his duel, together with the various provocations, which as a military man he was obliged to reſent; and declared his intention of demanding an impartial trial upon his arrival at Bombay, when I doubt not of his being honourably acquitted of every aſperſion which the malice of his enemies has wantonly thrown upon his character.

Joanna is ſituate between the N. W. ſide of the iſland of Madagaſcar, and the coaſt of Africa in forty five degrees of E. L. and twelve of S. L. It is a moſt commodious watering place for Eaſt Indiamen, the harbour being perfectly ſecure even in the moſt ſtormy weather, and the country abounding

abounding with provisions. Pine apples, water melons, oranges, mangoes, and all the fruits of the torrid zone are here in the highest perfection, and are so extremely cheap that the natives, who seem to have very little idea of the value of money, will readily give as much as would load a wheelbarrow in exchange for a blanket or an old shirt. They profess the Mahometan religion, and have a plurality of wives. Their king is a most absolute monarch, but governs his subjects with lenity and moderation. No crime is here punished with so much severity as theft, and yet I believe the children from their earliest infancy are taught to steal; a convincing proof that the severest laws are not the best calculated for the suppression of vice. The first offence is punished with the loss of the left hand; for the second the right is forfeited, and the third, however great the rank of the offender, is inevitable death. I saw several of these wretches who had suffered a single amputation, and one who had loſt both his hands, and yet was reckoned the moſt dexterous pick-pocket upon the iſland.

The crew of the ſhip-wrecked Indiaman are diſperſed upon the beach, ſome in temporary ſheds covered with remnants of the ſails, and ſome in huts built after the Indian faſhion, and thatched with the boughs of trees. The captain reſides in a houſe which was preſented to him by his majeſty, and is really much more habitable than could be expected from the rude hands of ſuch untutored workmen. The major part of the crew are to return to Europe in the homeward bound Indiaman; the principal officers, and about twenty of the men are to reviſit India with us, and poor Roche is to wait for ſome future opportunity of tranſporting himſelf to Bombay.

I had long foreſeen from the various broils which diſturbed the peace of our little government, that ſome very ſerious conſequences muſt enſue, and my obſervation

vation has been in ſome degree juſtified by a moſt curious and I believe unexampled duel (if a duel it may be called) which took place yeſterday between the young Hibernian of whom I made honourable mention in a former letter, and the ſecond officer of our ſhip, in conſequence of a box which in the heat of argument the latter had rather haſtily applied to the ear of the cadet. Seven in the evening was the hour appointed for this tremendous combat, and we were all impatient for the event, as the enraged Iriſhman had ſworn that he would ſatiate his fury with the blood of his antagoniſt, and rejoiced at the proſpect of once more ſacrificing a human victim to his injured honour. Both parties were punctual to the appointment and their ſeconds had taken care they ſhould be furniſhed with piſtols of no deſpicable length, and in caſe thoſe failed of the neceſſary execution, the matter was to be finally decided by the ſword. Every thing being now ſettled, the combatants were placed back to back, and were ordered to march five paces forward and then to turn round and fire. The ſailor, who ſeemed determined to pay the moſt implicit obedience to his ſecond, ſtalked with a ſlow and ſolemn ſtep the appointed number of paces, and turning round diſcharged his piſtol, when to his infinite aſtoniſhment he beheld the cadet far enough out of the reach of piſtol-ſhot, and exerting all his agility to gain a mangoe grove about three hundred yards diſtant from the field of battle. You may gueſs what a fund of entertainment this little accident has afforded us, and how many unpleaſant jeſts the Hibernian hero muſt in future undergo, who will ſtand in need of all his native impudence to ſupport ſuch complicated diſgrace.

LETTER. V.

Madraſs, Auguſt, 1774.

THE children of Iſrael, when releaſ-ed from their Babyloniſh captivity, could not have welcomed the happy hour of their deliverance with more exquiſite joy, than what I felt on the morning of the eighth, when we anchored in Mad-raſs roads and prepared ourſelves for a vi-ſit to Fort St. George, which is the prin-cipal of the company's ſettlements on the Coromandel coaſt, ſituate in 80 degrees of E. L. and thirteen of L, and from the natural beauties of its ſituation as well as the extreme healthineſs of the climate, is with juſtice ſtiled the Montpelier of the Eaſt. Our Captain, to whom I had lately rendered ſome trifling ſervices by ſupply-ing the place of ſecretary, now made very ample amends for that attention which I had paid to his affairs by the obliging offer of his houſe and table, while we ſhould remain on ſhore; a moſt fortunate circumſtance for me, who muſt otherwiſe have taken up my lodgings in a dirty punch-houſe.

On the ninth I accompanied the captain on ſhore, and the following morning I paid my compliments to the governor, who received me with great affability and politeneſs, and without any of that pompous ceremony, which I ſuppoſed inſeparable from oriental greatneſs. From the little I have hitherto ſeen, I feel myſelf highly prepoſſeſſed in favour of Madraſs. The elegance of the buildings, the beautiful rows of trees which form an agreeable ſhade on each ſide of the ſtreets, and the univerſal appearance of wealth and magnificence muſt ſtrike forcibly on the eyes of a ſtranger, and indeed have not in the leaſt diſappointed thoſe pleaſing ideas which I had formed of Aſiatic grandeur. The houſes of the Engliſh gentlemen are lofty

lofty and well proportioned, and from their construction are so extremely cool, that I can scarcely believe myself in the torrid zone. Every person who can afford it has a country retreat at the distance of a few miles, which is called a garden-house and is fitted up with peculiar elegance. The form of government here somewhat resembles an English corporation, all matters of law being referred to a court of mayor and aldermen, where justice is administred in a very summary way without any of that infamous chicanery and those oppressive delays which disgrace our courts in England. In religious matters here is a universal toleration. The Jew, the Christian, the disciple of Brahma, and the worshipper of Mahomet pursue each his favourite system, and no man seems inclined to dispute with his neighbour which is the easiest road to heaven.

At a short distance from the fort at a village called Triplicane resides the Nabob of Arcot, who is acknowleged an

ally

ally of the Britiſh empire, and is by the treaty of Paris an independent prince. He keeps a very ſplendid court, where the Engliſh meet with every mark of attention, and are often preferred to very lucrative poſts about his perſon. He has twelve battalions of foot, and ſeveral regiments of dragoons commanded by Engliſh officers, and tolerably well verſed in the European art of war. This prince has lately acquired a conſiderable addition to his territorial poſſeſſions by the capture of Tanjour (which with all its dependencies) ſurrendered to the united forces of the Nabob and company after an obſtinate ſiege of ſeveral months. The depoſed king is now a priſoner in that capital, which was once his own, and I ſuppoſe will ſoon fall a ſacrifice to that cruel policy of the Eaſt, which too often deprives an unfortunate monarch of his crown and life together. The prize money on this occaſion diſtributed to the

army

army amounted to an immenſe ſum, the ſhare of the commander in chief alone being calculated at one hundred thouſand pounds. The kingdom, of which Tanjour is the capital, lies about two hundred miles to the ſouth-weſt of Madraſs, being ſeparated from the iſland of Ceylon by a narrow channel, and was hitherto governed by a prince who was tributary to to the Great Mogul. The river Colleroon, which runs near the walls of Tanjour, at ſtated periods overflows, and fertilizes the land, as the Nile does that of Egypt. The waters are extremely rapid, and like thoſe of the Ganges are held ſacred by the natives. The capital of the Nabob's dominions is Arcot; a large and well fortified town near one hundred miles to the weſtward of Madraſs; but he has for ſome years paſt reſided entirely at Triplicane, where under the immediate protection of the Engliſh his perſon is ſecure from either foreign or domeſtic ene-

my,

my, and where he is at hand to influence the governor and council, as his own intereſt ſhall require, by the power of all-prevailing gold. He has three ſons, the ſecond of whom is his favorite, and is Captain General of his army.

LETTER VI.

Madrafs, Auguft, 1774.

I Yefterday dined at the Governor's public table, and fpent a moft agreeable evening at his garden-houfe. The dinner was elegant, the attendants numerous, and indeed every thing bore the appearance rather of regal fplendor, than of the domeftic eftablifhment of a governor, who is not even the reprefentative of a crowned head. We retired foon after dinner according to the cuftom of the country to take our afternoon's nap, which the heat of the climate renders abfolutely neceffary for the refrefhment of our bodies, which muft neceffarily be weakened by a continual perfpiration. In the evening I ordered my palanquin, that I might indulge myfelf with a view of the country previous to the hour of meeting at the governor's.

governor's. A palanquin is a couch covered with an arched canopy, and supported on the ſhoulders of men, a moſt luxurious mode of conveyance, I aſſure you, and well adapted to a country, where even the motion of a carriage is deemed too violent an exerciſe for the effeminate inhabitants. I found the appearance of the country extremely beautiful, the roads ſhaded by trees whoſe branches entirely exclude the rays of the ſun, and numberleſs little boxes interſperſed amidſt fields, and rice grounds, forming altogether the moſt elegant landſkip that can be conceived.

On my arrival at the governor's, where I found the company already aſſembled, I was moſt agreeably ſurpriſed at the ſight of ſeveral card-tables which were filled with Engliſh ladies, who though the ſun had rather tarniſhed their complexions ſtill retained charms ſufficient even to have capivated an eaſtern monarch. They were dreſſed in light muſlins,

the

the produce of the country, and ſeemed totally to have laid aſide that unbecoming ſtiffneſs, which too often contributes to diminiſh the charms of the Britiſh fair. Our entertainment was ſuperb, the wines were excellent, and a univerſal ſpirit of good humour and conviviality prevailed. Indeed I felt myſelf ſo perfectly at eaſe, and partook ſo heartily of the general mirth, that I believe I did not once in the whole evening devote a ſingle thought to my poor forſaken Charlotte. Do not however think me already inconſtant, or ſuppoſe that I have ſo ſoon baniſhed the remembrance of that dear girl from my breaſt. Her image is at this moment preſent to my eyes, and I think of the delicious moments which I have ſpent with her as of a fairy tale, or a dream never to be accompliſhed.

I this morning roſe before the ſun, and paid a viſit to the Black town which ſtands about a mile to the northward of the fort, and is inhabited by merchants from all the quarters of the globe. Its appearance when contrasted with that of fort St. George is mean and shabby, but still there are some tolerable streets, several churches handsomely decorated with the offerings of the superstitious, and some Pagodas or Indian temples. The habitations of the natives are low and ill-contrived, consisting generally of two or three dismal apartments surrounding a small court, their jealousy forbidding the use of windows, least the persons of their women should be polluted by the unhallowed eyes of strangers.

It is well known that in all countries priestcraft flourishes in proportion to the ignorance of the people, and no country affords a more ample field for it than India. Immense sums have been lavished by the Gentoos in building Pagodas and in offerings to their gods. Even their most beautiful women are consecrated to the church, and their virgin charms are rifled by the priests. They are called dancing

dancing girls, and they aſſiſt at all religious ceremonies, proceſſions, and at weddings. They are both by religion and profeſſion proſtitutes, being reſtricted from marrying, and obliged by vow to ſubmit to the embraces of every man of their own caſt or ſect, who ſhall requeſt the favour. They are much admired by the European gentlemen, whom they are very ready to oblige, as they find them ſo much more generous than their own countrymen.

The Mahometans, or as they are here called, the Moormen, are a very different race of people from the Gentoos. They are not originally natives of the country, but having formerly overrun it by force of arms, they ſtill keep poſſeſſion of what they won by their valour, nor will the puſillanimous Gentoos ever recover the loſt inheritance of their forefathers, till they have ſhaken off thoſe ſhackles which ſuperſtition and prieſtcraft have impoſed upon them. The Moormen are all ſoldiers of fortune, and their ſword is their religion. They boaſt that they derive their deſcent from the mighty Tamerlane, and to ſuch a pitch do they carry their veneration for their noble anceſtor, that they would puniſh the ſlighteſt word of diſreſpect againſt his name with the immediate death of the offender.

On the twentieth we ſhall re-embark, and proceed on our voyage to Bengal, where if I find the ſame hoſpitable manners and as much agreeable ſociety as I have experienced at Madraſs, I ſhall think the dangers of the voyage amply compenſated, and ſhall heartily congratulate myſelf on my arrival in a country, where amidſt the dazzling temptations of wealth the purſuit of riches is not ſuffered to interfere with the pleaſures of ſocial intercourſe.

LETTER VII.

Calcutta, Oct. 1774.

ON the tenth of laſt month we arrived in the river Hughley, and came to an anchor at Culpee, where a Budgeroe, or Indian boat ſomewhat reſembling a ſtate barge upon the Thames, attended from my friend Hancock to convey me to Calcutta. The navigation of the Hughley is extremely dangerous from the continual ſhifting of the ſands, and from the numerous ſhoals againſt which the ſhips are guarded by buoys placed at certain diſtances, and are directed by ſmall pilot ſloops, which at the company's expence conſtantly attend the Indiamen. On the banks of the river ſtands Fort William, which is conſiderably larger than Madraſs, and is garriſoned by an European regiment and by ſeveral companies of

Seapoys or native ſoldiers. About a mile farther is the town of Calcutta, which is near three leagues in circumference, and is ſo irregularly built, that it looks as if the houſes had been placed wherever chance directed, here the lofty manſion of an Engliſh chief, and there the thatched hovel of an Indian cooly. The Bezaars, or markets, which ſtand in the middle of the town, are ſtreets of miſerable huts, and every Indian who occupies one of theſe is called a merchant. There is a noble playhouſe, but no church, the want of which is ſupplied by a ſpacious apartment in the old fort, adjoining to the room ſo well known by the name of the black hole, and rendered famous by by the deaths of our unfortunate countrymen, when the Nabob Surajah Dowlah took Calcutta by ſtorm. An Engliſh lady, who ſaw her huſband periſh at her feet, ſurvived that miſerable cataſtrophe, and the tyrant was ſo captivated with her beauty, that he promoted her to the honour

nour of his bed, and ſhe remained ſeven years in his ſeraglio, when ſhe was releaſed at the requeſt of governor Vanſittart, and is now alive at Calcutta.

You know I went out particularly recommended to Mr. Hancock, whom I formerly knew in England, and whoſe lady is my near relation. I want words to expreſs my gratitude for the favours with which this gentleman has loaded me. He has given me an apartment in his houſe, has furniſhed me with a ſuperfluity of all the articles of dreſs, &c. and even granted me an unlimited order for money on his Sarcar or caſh-bearer. You will perhaps laugh at the idea of caſh-bearer, but I aſſure you in this country no gentleman takes the trouble of keeping his own money. It is entruſted to the Sarcar, whoſe friends are reſponſible for his honeſty, and to him all tradeſmens bills, and demands for the current expences of the houſe are preſented the firſt of every month. This man is under the controul of the Banyan

or

or head ſteward, who hires and diſcharges all inferior domeſtics at his pleaſure, and is the agent in all commercial concerns. I have been preſented to the governor general by Mr. Hancock, who has been for many years on terms of the moſt intimate friendſhip with him, and to whoſe recommendation he never fails of paying immediate attention. The manners of Mr. Haſtings are extremely engaging, and his deportment totally void of that oſtentatious pride, which too often throws a ſhade over the virtues of thoſe men, in whom ſuch ſupreme authority is veſted. He poſſeſſes a great fund of claſſical learning, and is perfect maſter of the Oriental languages. But the moſt amiable part of his character is his attention to the diſtreſſes of the indigent. To him the widow and the fatherleſs never apply in vain for relief, nor has he ever been known to withhold the pitying hand of charity from thoſe objects, whoſe poverty has been the effect of misfortune and not of vice. I have

have received the moſt flattering aſſuran-ces from him that ſome proviſion ſhall be made for me in the military line, and I underſtand from my friend, that it is the intention of the governor to procure me a lucrative appointment in the ſervice of the Nabob of Oude. At preſent I ſhall con-tine to reſide with Mr. Hancock, whoſe general knowledge of mankind renders him a moſt agreeable companion, and who though upwards of fifty years of age ſtill retains all the fire and pleaſantry of youth.

The principal diverſions of Calcutta are balls, card parties, and what are cal-led the Europe ſhops, which are literally magazines of every European article ei-ther of luxury or convenience. Theſe early in the morning are the public ren-dezvous of the idle and the gay, who here propagate the ſcandal of the day, and pur-chaſe at an immoderate price the toys of Mr. Pinchbeck and the frippery of Tavi-ſtock-ſtreet. In the evening the roads for ſeveral miles round the town are filled with

with chariots, whiſkeys, and phaetons, each horſe being attended by a naked black, who trots cloſe to the carriage covered with ſweat and duſt. The palanquins are like the ſedan chairs in England, but carried on the ſhoulders of men, who ſing a moſt unmelodious ſong as they run along with their burthen.

Moſt of the gentlemen, who have reſided any length of time in India, are much addicted to the Hooka, a moſt curious machine for ſmoaking tobacco through water, the ſmoke being conveyed by a tube of amazing length which is called a ſnake, and is waſhed with roſe-water. Even the writers, whoſe ſalary and perquiſites ſcarce amount to two hundred pounds a year, contrive to be attended wherever they go by their Hooka-burdaar, or ſervant whoſe duty it is to repleniſh the Hooka with the neceſſary ingredients, and to keep up the fire with his breath. But extravagant as the Engliſh are in their Hooka, their equipage, and

and their tables, yet all this is abſolute parſimony, when compared to the expences of a ſeraglio; a luxury which only thoſe can enjoy, whoſe rank in the ſervice entitles them to a princely income, and whoſe Haram, like the ſtate horſes of a monarch, is conſidered as a neceſſary appendage to Eaſtern grandeur. However you would think even this extravagance in ſome degree pardonable, had you once experienced the attractive charms of an Aſiatic beauty. I have ſeen ladies of the Gentoo caſt, ſo exquiſitely formed, with limbs ſo divinely turned, and ſuch expreſſion in their eyes, that if you can reconcile yourſelf to their complexions you muſt acknowledge them not inferior to the moſt celebrated beauties of Europe. For my own part, I already begin to think the dazzling brightneſs of a copper-coloured face infinitely preferable to the pallid and ſickly hue, which baniſhes the roſes from the cheeks of the European fair, and reminds me of the death-ſtruck counten-

ance

ance of Lazarus risen from the grave. The English ladies are immoderately fond of dancing, an exercise ill calculated for the burning climate of Bengal, and in my opinion, however admissible in cooler latitudes, not a little indelicate in a country, where the inhabitants are covered with no more cloaths than what decency absolutely requires. Imagine to yourself the lovely object of your affections ready to expire with heat, every limb trembling and every feature distorted with fatigue, and her partner with a muslin handkerchief in each hand employed in the delightful office of wiping down her face, while the big drops stand impearled upon her forehead; and then ask your own heart, if an Indian damsel just risen from the limpid bath, in all the native charms of cleanliness and artless beauty, is not much more likely to inspire you with sentiments of desire and love.

LETTER VIII.

Calcutta, Dec. 1774.

WHEN I laſt wrote to my dear friend, I had flattered myſelf with the hopes of being ſpeedily fixed in a ſituation, which would have been attended with conſiderable pleaſure as well as profit, as I had promiſed myſelf an inexauſtible fund of entertainment from viſiting the interior parts of India. Theſe hopes were at firſt delayed by a violent inflammation of the liver, which for three weeks confined me to my bed, and are now totally cut off by the arrival of the newly appointed members of the ſupreme council, who uniformly oppoſe every meaſure that Mr. Haſtings recommends, and thus effectually deprive his dependants of that proviſion, which they look ed up to from his goodneſs and liberality. I am now ſo weak that I can ſcarcely hold my pen, and I aſſure you that the Knight of La Mancha could not boaſt a more woeful countenance, than what my looking glaſs now exhibits to my view. I attribute my diſorder to certain acts of intemperance which I have committed contrary to the advice of Mr. Hancock, who moſt kindly repreſented to me the fatal conſequences of filling too many bumpers to the health of my abſent friends. However I am now taught a leſſon by which I hope to profit in future, and ſhall henceforward be a better œconomiſt of my conſtitution. I think the old proverb, which ſays that misfortunes ſeldom come ſingly, is now verified in me. I have received a letter from my father, reprobating in ſevere terms my attachment to Miſs Rivers, and painting in the ſtrongeſt colours the folly of ſuch romantic engagements. I confeſs his opinion in ſome degree to be juſt, but I wiſh that his letter had been couched in more gentle terms. The ſame ſhip brought me me alſo a packet from my Charlotte, by which I underſtand that I had ſcarcely ſailed from England before her old admirer at the grove renewed his addreſſes to her, and that her father ſeemed very much inclined to countenance them. Mr. Rivers had not yet in plain terms declared his ſentiments, but had juſt hinted to her the uncertainty of my return from India; talked of the natural inconſtancy of young men; and dwelt much on the happineſs of that woman, who ſhould be ſo fortunate as to engage the affections of Mr. Greville. Her letter is filled with alternate expreſſions of hope and fear, her concern at not hearing from me from every place where ſhe imagines we touched during the voyage, and ends as it began with eternal vows of love and conſtancy.

Such is the preſent ſituation of my affairs. My family is diſpleaſed with me, I have already loſt my hopes of promotion in Bengal, and am likely to loſe my miſtreſs at home. Mr. Hancock advifes me to return to Madrafs, where the recommendations of Mr. Haftings to the governor of Fort St. George cannot fail of procuring me a commiffion, and where I may gather perhaps a greater quantity of military laurels than of fterling gold. As foon as my health is perfectly re-eftablifhed, I believe I fhall take his advice, for I fee very little profpect of fucceeding here, as the numerous dependants, which have arrived in the train of the judges, and of the new commander in chief of the forces, will of courfe be appointed to all the pofts of any emolument, and I muft do thofe gentlemen the juftice to obferve that both in number and rapacity they exactly refemble an army of locufts fent to devour the fruits of the earth.

The inhabitants of Calcutta feem to be not a little difpleafed at the new form of government, which the judges, or as they call themfelves the fupreme court of judicature

dicature in Bengal, have already began to introduce. The mayor's court is abolished, and the same legal process which is used at Westminster now prevails. The attornies, who have followed the judges in search of prey, as the carrion crows do an Indian army on its march, are extremely successful in supporting the spirit of litigation among the natives, who like children delighted with a new play-thing, are highly pleased with the opportunity of harrassing one another by vexatious suits; and those pests of society called bailiffs, a set of miscreants hitherto little known in India, are now to be seen in every street watching for the unhappy victims devoted to legal persecution. Even the menial servants are now tutored to breathe that insolent spirit of English licentiousness, which teaches the slave to insult his master, and then bring his action of damages at Westminster, if deservedly chastised for his impudence. Arbitrary fines are daily imposed on gentlemen who preſume to correct their ſlaves; and the houſe of the chief juſtice of Bengal reſembles the office of a trading magiſtrate in Weſtminſter, who decides the ſquabbles of oyſter-women, and picks up a livelihood by the ſale of ſhilling warrants.

LETTER IX.

Calcutta, April, 1775.

THE ſame untoward deſtiny, which has hitherto blaſted all my proſpects, has ſtill purſued me, and I have within the ſhort ſpace of a few revolving months experienced all the variegated miſery of ſickneſs, ſhipwreck, captivity, and hunger. Finding my views in Bengal ſo cruelly diſappointed, and hoping that the recommendations of the governor-general would procure me a permanent eſtabliſhment at Madraſs, on Chriſtmas day I bid adieu to my generous benefactor, and embarked on board a country veſſel, ſo called in contradiſtinction to the ſhips of Europe, and navigated by Laſcars, or Indian ſailors. We fell down the river without any accident, and the ſeaſon of the year being not unfavourable, our commander, who had been many years in the

the ſervice and was perfectly acquainted with the navigation of the Indian ſeas, flattered us with the agreeable proſpect of a ſpeedy voyage to Madraſs. However, that ruling deſtiny, which preſides over the events of this world, had ordained it otherwiſe, and I was doomed to meet with every aggravated diſtreſs, which a tempeſtuous ſea and an inhoſpitable ſhore could heap upon me.

On the thirtieth of december our pilot left us, and we congratulated ourſelves on our eſcape from the ſhoals and quickſands ſo dangerous to inexperienced navigators in the mouth of the Ganges. On the firſt of January about ſeven in the evening the wind freſhened ſo much, and the ſky bore ſo threatening an appearance, that the captain thought it neceſſary to take in part of his ſails and prepare for the approaching gale. Before five the next morning it blew a perfect hurricane, and in a few hours more the Laſcars, who are active enough in fine weather but are moſt

egregious

egregious cowards in the moment of danger, were so overpowered with fatigue and terror that they forsook the deck, nor could all the endeavours of the captain, who remonstrated, begged, and even threatened them with immediate death, bring them back to their duty. In this situation, while the waves broke incessantly over the deck and swept away every thing before them, we remained at the mercy of the elements till about two in the morning of the third, when the vessel struck with such violence upon the ground that the masts went overboard, the lower parts of the ship were filled with water, and we set almost petrified in the cabbin in momentary expectation of being launched into eternity. Under these shocking circumstances, nearly suffocated with the water which poured in upon us, and trembling least the ship should part from the violence with which she thumped, we remained till the dawn of day, when with difficulty we crawled upon the deck, and discovered land

land at the diſtance of about ſix leagues ſurrounded by breakers, and ſeeming to tantalize us with a view of that ſafety which we imagined beyond our reach. However the captain, whoſe reſolution throughout this trying ſcene had never forſaken him, now recommended to us to exert all our ſtrength in preparing a raft, which might convey thoſe on ſhore whom the only remaining boat could not contain, and he entreated us not to neglect this opportunity which Providence had offered for our relief, while the ſhip ſhould hang together. Animated by his example we laboured with all the diligence of men ſtruggling for their lives, and ſoon completed a raft of ſuch booms and maſts as the ſea had ſpared us, and launched it upon the waves. On this aukward machine, ſo haſtily put together, and faſtened only with ropes we embarked twenty-ſix in number, and committed ourſelves to the ocean. In leſs than ten minutes we ſaw the boat, which the Laſcars had loaded ed to the water's edge, overwhelmed by a mountainous wave, and almoſt at the ſame inſtant the ſhip went to pieces, and the wretched part of the crew who, ſtupified with deſpair had awaited their fate upon the deck, were buried in one watery grave. It was not a ſeaſon for us to lament the fate of others. We each moment expected to ſhare the ſame deſtiny, having neither ſail nor paddle to direct our raft, when a huge ſurf overſet the unwieldy machine, and twelve of our companions ſunk to riſe no more. The reſt with infinite difficulty regained the raft, which being now conſiderably lightened, the wind blew us gradually towards the ſhore, where about half an hour before ſun-ſet we landed almoſt fainting with fatigue and hunger, and our limbs ſo benumbed with cold, that we were utterly unable to ſeek for a place of ſhelter either from the inclemency of the weather, or from the fury of thoſe beaſts, which we apprehend-

ed

ed would prove leſs merciful to us than the ocean which we had juſt eſcaped from.

Our fears however proved groundleſs, and we recruited our waſted ſpirits by a profound ſleep uninterrupted by the viſitors which we ſo much dreaded, and whoſe preſence afterwards became more familiar to us. Our firſt object in the morning was to diſcover a ſpring of freſh water, that we might allay our thirſt, through which we had ſuffered conſiderably during the laſt four and twenty hours. This we were fortunate enough to accompliſh, and we then commenced our journey along the ſea-ſhore, and after travelling about two leagues arrived on the banks of a river, the water of which we found brackiſh and unpalatable. Here we obſerved the footſteps of men, and from the ſmoke which we perceived iſſuing from amidſt the trees in a neighbouring grove, we juſtly concluded that we ſhould find an Indian village. As our circumſtances admitted of no heſitation, we marched boldly on, and after purſuing the tract for about a mile we arrived at a ſpot covered with a few paltry huts, the inhabitants of which fled precipitately at our approach, notwithſtanding our tokens of ſubmiſſion, and the wretched appearance of our defenceleſs company, which was more calculated to inſpire pity than terror. However as our appetites became rather preſſing, we took poſſeſſion of their huts without ceremony, where we found abundance of rice and ſeveral earthen veſſels filled with the liquor of the cocoa-nut, which proved a moſt comfortable meal to poor creatures, who had actually kept a moſt rigid faſt for at leaſt three days. We had ſcarcely finiſhed our breakfaſt, and were forming our future plan of operations, when we were alarmed by the ſound of horns, trumpets, and ſeveral other uncouth inſtruments which the Indians make uſe of when they go to battle, and peeping out of our hiding places we found ourſelves ſurrounded by at leaſt five hundred men armed with matchlocks, pikes, ſabres, and bows of an amazing length. We immediately implored their mercy and protection by the moſt ſubmiſſive geſtures, and fortunately a Laſcar ſpeaking the language of the country explained to them the circumſtances of our ſhipwreck, and aſſured them they ſhould be moſt liberally rewarded, if they would conduct us to the neareſt Engliſh ſettlement. An elderly Indian, who from the reſpect which the reſt paid him appeared to be their chief, aſſured us of his protection, and ordered us to be conducted to a hovel on the outſkirts of the village, where we were deſired by our guards to repoſe ourſelves, and were permitted the honour of ſitting down among their oxen, which in India are uſed as beaſts of burthen, and enjoy at leaſt as comfortable habitations as their maſters. They did not however omit the previous ceremony of ſtripping us of every thing valuable we had about us. Our watches, buckles, and what little money we had in our pockets were ſoon taken from us with as much avidity and as little ceremony as if we had been caſt away on the weſtern coaſt of England, and fallen into the hands of the humane inhabitants of Cornwall.

We found that the fatal ſpot, where our ſhip and the major part of her unhappy crew had periſhed, was called Carrica Bay, ſituate midway between Point Palmyra and Falſe Point, places well known to the Indian navagators, and like Charybdis of old rendered famous by the deſtruction of unfortunate mariners. We were now reduced to the miſerable ſituation of ſubſiſting on the charity of ſavages, naked, helpleſs, and imploring the pity of the inhabitants of that once happy country, whoſe provinces have been deſolated, and whoſe ſons have ſo oft been ſacrificed on the altars of European avarice. However our captivity was not of long continuance; a Laſcar having found the means to eſcape to Balaſore, where he communicated the

 particulars

particulars of our diſtreſs to the Engliſh reſident, and convinced him of the neceſſity of taking ſome ſpeedy meaſures for our relief. Mr. Marriot, whoſe humanity and benovolence I ſhall ever acknowledge in the higheſt terms of gratitude, made immediate application to the Rajah of Catack, then in alliance with the company, to whoſe authority our maſters were in ſome degree ſubject, and procured an order for our releaſe, and for a guard to attend us to Balaſore. I believe little attention would have been paid to this order, had not Mr. Marriot prudently hinted to the Rajah the conſequence of the governor-general's diſpleaſure, ſhould the ſervants of the company be detained or ill-treated in thoſe diſtricts over which he preſided. This had its proper effect upon the Rajah, who took ſuch effectual ſteps to reſtore us to our liberty, that on the twenty ſixth of February we were permitted to proceed on our journey, and were eſcorted by a body of

men

men ſufficient to protect us from inſults upon the road. Our little company was now reduced to four Europeans, and ſix Laſcars, the ſecond mate of the ſhip having fallen a martyr to fatigue and ſickneſs; Mr. Edwards, a writer on the Madraſs eſtabliſhment, a moſt amiable young man, and who deſerved a better fate, having expired in the greateſt agonies from the bite of a ſnake; and a Portugueze ſurgeon having ſuddenly diſappeared, whether after the example of the Laſcar he eſcaped to ſome neighbouring ſettlement, or was devoured by tygers in the woods, we never learnt. We proceeded by eaſy marches through a country beautiful by nature, but utterly deſtitute of cultivation, and for the firſt three days met with no accident that could interrupt our tranquillity, or diminiſh the joy we felt at our approaching deliverance. On the morning of the fourth as we travelled along the ſide of a large wood, the chief mate unfortunately loitering behind, and perhaps careleſs from the ſecurity of the preceding days, was ſeized by a tyger that had lurked beneath a thicket, and was carried inſtantly from our view in ſpite of all our endeavours and the united efforts of our guard to ſave him. It is remarkable that this unhappy man had ever treated the Laſcars under his command with ſuch ſeverity, that his name inſpired them with terror. It was believed, that more than one had died through his cruelty, and during the few days which preceded our ſhipwreck he had omitted no opportunity of chaſtiſing theſe inoffenſive creatures for the moſt trifling fault. I ſincerely pitied him in the moment of his untimely death, but I think I ſhall not be deemed uncharitable if I expreſs a wiſh, that every tyrant may meet a ſimilar fate. For where ſhall the oppreſſor of his fellow-creatures find ſo proper a tomb, as in the maw of the moſt ferocious of the brute creation?

During the reft of our journey we met with no other inconvenience than what muft neceffarily arife from fatigue, and from the want of fhoes to protect our feet from the loofe ftones of which the roads were full, and on the fixteenth of March arrived fafe at Balafore. Here we were entertained with every poffible mark of attention by Mr. Marriot, who furnifhed us with wearing apparel in great abundance, and politely infifted on our remaining a few days with him, that we might at his hofpitable table recover health and fpirits to profecute our journey to Calcutta. We fpent a moft agreeable week with this worthy gentleman, to whom I fhall ever hold myfelf indebted for my deliverance from captivity and death, and then embarked in a fmall floop for Calcutta, which we reached without any accident, to the furprize and joy of our friends, who had fuppofed us buried in the ocean, and now received us as men rifen from the grave. My obligations to

Mr.

Mr. Hancock on this occaſion are beyond the power of words to expreſs. He had with unfeigned ſorrow lamented my untimely end, and he now welcomed my return to life and liberty with tears of ſincere affection. The governor-general too, whoſe generous heart ever feels for the diſtreſſes of the unfortunate, in the politeſt terms congratulated me on my deliverance, and renewed his offer of recommendations to Madraſs.

In a very few days I ſhall again tempt the faithleſs ocean, but ſhall previouſly appeaſe the god of tempeſts by frequent libations of Mr. Hancock's claret, which I believe to be full as acceptable an offering as the celebrated Falernum of the ancients.

LETTER X.

Madrass, June, 1775.

MY dearest friend's letter, which I received a few days after my arrival at Madrass, has given me the highest satisfaction. Indeed I know of no pleasure equal to that of hearing from an absent friend, and enjoying that mutual intercourse of sentiments, of which even the vast expanse of ocean, that divides us, cannot rob us. Your interview with my father, whose goodness of heart has ever been conspicuous, tho' sometimes the violence of his passions may rise superior to his natural benevolence, will I doubt not be productive of the desired advantage to me. His resentment will of course subside, when the cause from which it sprang has ceased, and the marriage of Miss Rivers, which I suppose my next packet will announce, will obliterate the remembrance

of

of every paſt folly. I aſſure you, I blame not Miſs Rivers. I accuſe her not of broken vows, nor do I invoke the offended god of love to puniſh the inconſtant fair. The days of romantic courtſhip have long been over, and Arcadian ſcenes of cottage felicity have loſt their charms. I think ſhe has diſplayed no little judgment in preferring a preſent eſtabliſhment to a future uncertain proſpect, and I moſt ſincerely wiſh her happy.

My own ſituation begins already to afford me the moſt flattering proſpect. I arrived at this agreeable place on the thirtieth of laſt month after a paſſage of five weeks, which at this time of the year is far from tedious. I reſide at preſent with Mr. Adams, who is maſter intendant at Fort St. George, and has, beſides the houſe allowed him by the Company, a moſt elegant little manſion in the pariſh of St. Thomas, about a league diſtant from Madraſs. To the governor of Madraſs I wanted no introduction, as I had on my firſt arrival

arrival at India the honour of being presented to him, and the letter which I now brought from Mr. Hastings ensured me a favourable reception. However my expectations from this quarter I knew to be inconsiderable, as an ensigncy in the Company's service was the most I had a right to expect, or indeed was in the power of the governor to bestow. This however was not to be refused, and a commission has been given me with the pay of five shillings a day, an income not only insufficient to procure the luxuries of life, but even greatly inadequate to the common necessaries. From general Joseph Smith, commander in chief of the forces on this coast, I had further views, and in these I have fortunately sueceeded. I have mentioned to you in a former letter that the Nabob of Arcot had several regiments commanded by European Officers, whose salaries were considerable, and whose emoluments from the nature of their commands, far removed from the capital, and

subject

ſubject only to military law, muſt be very great; an appointment under this prince appeared to me to be no deſpicable object, nor did I heſitate to prefer the ſervice of an Indian monarch to the honour, however great it may be deemed, of carrying arms in the employment of a trading company. General Smith approved of my intentions, and introduced me in ſuch terms to the Nabob, that I have been at once promoted to the command of a troop of horſe, and I am now a conſtant attendant at the Durbar, till I ſhall receive orders to join my corps, which is encamped near two hundred miles to the Southward of Madraſs, on the banks of the river Colleroon.

From the ſhort viſit which I before paid to Madraſs I had entertained the moſt favourable ideas of a place, whoſe inhabitants I found ſo perfectly ſociable with each other and ſo truly hoſpitable to ſtrangers. I am happy to ſay that a nearer view has not in the ſmalleſt degree altered

my

my ſentiments, or induced me to feel any other regret for the ſettlement which I have left, than what gratitude naturally inſpires me with for the loſs of a friend, to whoſe kind exertions I owe my preſent fortunate ſituation.

Under the friendly roof of Mr. Adams I enjoy all the luxuries of life in a moſt unlimited degree. I have horſes and ſervants at my command, a palanquin when the heat renders the exerciſe of riding inconvenient, and I have free acceſs to the palace of the Nabob, who is uncommonly affable in his manners, and poſſeſſes none of that ferocity which we ſuppoſe inſeparable from a deſpotic monarch of the Eaſt, who too frequently wades to an uſurped throne thro' the blood of his predeceſſor, and whom the pleaſures of the Haram and the intoxicating gratification of ſenſual appetites render in his turn an eaſy victim to an ambitious miniſter and a venal ſoldiery.

The nature of a despotic government is in all countries nearly the same. The monarch is above the law, and so long as he can support his authority, his subjects bow submissive to his tyrannic nod; but his power depends on the fidelity of his guards, and he is himself the slave of that very army which he uses as the instrument of oppression and of arbitrary sway.

The army of an Eastern despot is controulled only by its own interest or caprice, and so were once the mighty legions of Rome. No sooner was the senate roused by a spirit of liberty and by a sense of its former greatness, than the sword of the Preætorian bands crushed suddenly the aspiring emulation. A dissolute soldiery thrust imperial Galba from the throne, when Rome was the unrivalled mistress of the world: and Nadir Shaw, a mere adventurer, carried fire and sword into the heart of India, and obliged even the great Mogul to tremble on his throne.

LETTER XI.

Madras, July, 1775.

MAhomet Alley, Nabob of Arcot and of the Carnatic, is defcended from a Tartar family. His anceftors were among thofe bold adventurers, who difdained to dwell in the humble tents of their native country, and who found it by no means difficult to ufurp the thrones of pufillanimous Gentoo princes, by their natural inactivity and by the invincible fhackles of fuperftition rendered an eafy prey to each foreign invader. Their belief of the Pythagorean doctrine forbids their fhedding the blood of the meaneft reptile that exifts, and though they will patiently endure the approach of death from a full perfuafion that they fhall reanimate fome other body, yet they will not exert themfelves in the defence of their lives and property; a fufficient proof, that felfpreſervation is not univerſally the firſt law of nature.

The Nabob has three ſons, the eldeſt of whom, Omdit Ul Omrah, is of a mild diſpoſition, totally loſt in the pleaſures of the ſeraglio, and is indeed little more than a ſtate priſoner in his own palace. The ſecond, Ameer Ul Omrah, who is the favourite of his father, is inveſted with the ſupreme military command, and to him chiefly the English pay their court. He is enterpriſing, deceitful, and unprincipled, and would long ago have embrued his hands in the blood of his family, had not his father, rendered wiſe by experience, removed his court from Arcot, and reſided under the immediate protection of the governor and council of Madraſs. The Nabob well knew how little the ſacred names of parent and of brother avail to reſtrain an aſpiring tyrant, and he was aware that the crime of the deteſted parricide is ſoon loſt in the pomp and ſplendor which ſurround the ſucceſsful monarch.

The

The youngeſt of the royal offspring is called Zapharah Mulk, and is educated among the women of the ſeraglio, where from his earlieſt infancy he is taught to imbibe the ſeeds of vice, and whence at the age of manhood he will emerge in a ſtate of the moſt deplorable ignorance.

The revenues of the Nabob ariſe from the rents of the country, which is parcelled out in diſtricts to his viceroys, and by them let in ſmaller diviſions to petty governors, who at their pleaſure diſtribute them to the farmers, allowing to each ſuch a proportion as he can find the means to cultivate. The farmers, after they have gathered in their grain, pay to the collectors of the revenues a ſum equal to one third of the original produce of the land, and theſe taxes are exacted with ſuch ſeverity, and without the ſmalleſt regard to a bad crop or to any of the unforeſeen accidents which diſtreſs the huſbandman, that it is a matter of aſtoniſhment to me how the poor Indian can pay his rent, and ſupport his family. You may judge what a climax of oppreſſion this form of government muſt give room to. The renters according to their different degrees of authority oppreſs each other, and the Nabob ſeldom fails of extorting conſiderable ſums from the principal to whom an invitation to court, is the certain ſignal that he muſt refund his ill gotten wealth, and deliver up to his rapacious maſter thoſe treaſures, which by a cruel gradation of tyranny have been ſqueezed from the induſtrious labourer.

How far the Brahmins, who are now the magi of the Eaſt, may be right in their chronology, I will not pretend to ſay. They trace back the hiſtory of Indoſtan to the reign of an emperor, who flouriſhed two thouſand years before the birth of Chriſt, and whoſe poſterity ſat fifteen centuries upon the throne, when the ſupineneſs of ſome luxurious monarch induced the diſaffected nobles to rebel, who like the generals of Alexander the Great divided

ded the empire among themſelves, and raiſed up ſeparate kingdoms of their own. This afforded an opening to the wandering tribes of Tartary, and to thoſe ambitious captains of the Perſian army, who inured to the hardſhips of the field, and thirſting after plunder, poured like a fierce torrent over the provinces of India, and eaſily ſubdued a people weakened by inteſtine broils, and enervated by eaſe and luxury.

You will here aſk how the Gentoos, whom I have deſcribed as equally incapable of defending themſelves as of invading the rights of others, came to forget their principles and their caſt, and to engage in the purſuits of war. I ſhould have informed you, that the fighting caſt, of which the Rajahpoots and the Mahrattas are the chief, are an exception to this rule. The former of theſe originally compoſed the body-guards of their princes, whence they derive their name; and the latter are a moſt formidable nation, inhabiting

biting the coaſt of Malabar, and extending acroſs the Peninſula of India almoſt to the Coromandel coaſt. They bring into the field numerous armies mounted on fleet and beautiful horſes, and they mark their footſteps by the moſt ſhocking ſcenes of plunder and devaſtation. Indoſtan has frequently ſuffered from their encroachments, and even the force of European diſcipline has hardly reſtrained the violence of theſe invaders, who ruſh upon their foe without order or regularity, like a herd of warlike animals armed by the ſole hand of nature, and are as expeditious in their retreat as they are furious in their firſt attack.

LETTER XII.

Madrass, July, 1775.

I Yesterday saw a most extroardinary instance of the power which superstition has over the human mind. Returning from the Durbar, I perceived in a field adjoining to the road a croud of people assembled round a man, who was suspended by the heels from a kind of gallows, and was swinging backwards and forwards over a slow fire. I enquired what crime he had committed to merit so curious a punishment, and was informed that he was a holy man, who had devoted himself to the service of the Almighty, and had made a solemn vow that he would daily undergo this voluntary penance, till it should please the supreme being to receive him into the mansions of the happy. I find these acts of mortification are very frequent, and the credulous Indians are taught

taught by their priests to believe that the antic tricks of a wretch quivering under self-inflicted tortures are an offering highly acceptable to god.

I have at last been honoured with my leave of audience, and shall in a few days bid adieu to Madrass. I have already prepared every thing for my journey, have arranged my domestic establishment, and I anticipate the joy I shall feel when mounted on an Arabian charger at the head of my whiskered troopers, whose courage I hope will fully correspond with their ferocious looks. I have seen detachments from several of the regiments, and I assure you their appearance is truly martial. The infantry I cannot say much in praise of. They are usually twelve months in arrears, and of course their officers cannot enforce that regularity of discipline, which can only be kept up in the armies of a prince, who condescends to be punctual in his payments.

The garrison of Fort St. George consists of several companies of English infantry, a respectable body of artillery, and a battalion of Seapoys, who endure that fatigue in the field, under which European constitutions would sink, and who have in various engagements displayed a perseverance and resolution that would do honour to the most hardy veterans. Their pay, which considering the cheapness of rice on which an Indian almost entirely subsists is more than equal to all their wants, is given them without any deduction on the first of every month, nor do the officers lie under those stoppages so injurious to the British army, which enrich the agent or the pay-master, while the unfortunate subaltern is deprived of a mite of that scanty subsistence so inadequate to the necessary expences of a gentleman.

LETTER XIII.

LETTER XIII.

Chillingbrum, Sept. 1775.

I Am at laſt comfortably ſettled in my new quarters, which I reached the eighteenth day after I left Fort St. George. My route extended along the ſea-coaſt, but was not diverſified by that variety of proſpect ſo ornamental to the environs of Madraſs; nor did I find the country ſo populous or ſo well cultivated as I expected. I ſpent two days at Pondicherry, the principal ſettlement belonging to the French in India, but containing little worthy the attention of a traveller. The fort appears to be ſtrong, and the works are numerous. The garriſon conſiſts of a battalion of the king's troops, and about fifteen hundred ſeapoys. From Pondicherry I proceeded to Cuddalore, a fort of conſiderable extent but in a moſt ſhattered condition, ſituate on the moſt beautiful ſpot in India, and diſtant about a mile from the ruins of Fort St. David's, which at the cloſe of the laſt war was given up to the French, and the fortifications levelled with the ground. I was here moſt politely entertained by Captain Harcourt Woodhouſe, formerly of the county of Hertfordſhire, who, after having ſpent a conſiderable fortune in every ſpecies of faſhionable diſſipation, entered into the ſervice of the Company; and though in his ſeventieth year ſtill retains a great ſhare of that activity and vigour, for which he was diſtinguiſhed in his youthful days. From Cuddalore I travelled by eaſy journeys to the plains of Chillingbrum, where our regiment is cantoned on the ſkirts of a pleaſant village, having a ſmall river in the rear, and a beautiful proſpect of woods, rice fields, and lofty pagodas in the front.

What is here called a regiment of cavalry, but which would more properly bear the name of legion, conſiſts of ſix troops

troops of dragoons, to which four companies of infantry and one of artillery are attached, with four light field pieces, which have lately been drawn by horſes, contrary to the cuſtom of the Mahometans, who from time immemorial have uſed oxen and buffaloes for draught, and whoſe obſtinacy ſeldom permits them to get the better of an eſtabliſhed prejudice. This corps is commanded by one European captain, two lieutenants, and ſix cornets, as field officers and captains, and under them by ſubadars and jemadars, who do the duty of ſubalterns, and who are men of high military reputation, as they riſe only by their merit, and are obliged to go through each ſubordinate ſtation before they attain the rank of officer. The infantry is under the ſeparate command of two ſubalterns, and the artillery under a lieutenant fire worker. Each regiment is attended by its own Bezaar or travelling market, which conſiſts of a long ſtreet of ſhops, that pay a ſmall tax to the commanding officer.

The police of the Bezaar is regulated by a Cutwall or magiſtrate of the market, who ſettles the price of proviſions and the exchange of money, and inflicts arbitrary puniſhments on ſuch perſons as are convicted of frauds, or offend againſt the eſtabliſhed rules of the Bezaar. The money-changers, who are mentioned in holy writ to have been driven out of the temple, are to be found in every part of India. Their cuſtoms have been handed down unaltered to the preſent hour, and their principles are not in the leaſt changed for the better. They are extremely dexterous in impoſing bad money on the ignorant, and if detected in the attempt, they moſt impudently deny the fact, and with great fluency of abuſe retort their charge upon the accuſer.

The introduction of modern diſcipline into the Indian armies has been the work of infinite labour and difficulty, and the Nabob of Arcot is the only prince who has yet brought it to the leaſt perfection. The even ranks into which European ſoldiers

ſoldiers form themſelves, the uninterrupted gradation of obedience from the chief commander down to the private man, and that regular order in which they march into battle, and which they preſerve even in the heat of action, appeared to the untutored Indians as the effects of magic; and they conſidered thoſe men who could undaunted expoſe themſelves to certain death, and who coolly filled up each interval when the murdering cannon had ſwept away half their ranks, as beings of an order ſuperior to the common race of mortals, whom it was equally impoſſible either to reſiſt or imitate. Experience however has taught them the contrary, and they now acknowledge the force of diſcipline, and are ſenſible that the moſt deſtructive weapons are uſeleſs in the hands of men who diſdain the aſſiſtance of art, and like the ferocious inhabitants of their native woods repoſe a blind confidence in that courage, which only leads them to more certain ruin.

LETTER XIV.

Chillingbrum, October, 1775.

I Am juſt returned from an expedition againſt a party of Collories, or ſavage banditti, inhabiting the ſpacious woods which extend through the greateſt part of the Carnatic, and who live by the plunder of ſuch unfortunate travellers as fall into their hands, and often in large bodies attack thoſe villages which they know to be unprotected by ſeapoys. Servants who have robbed their maſters, deſerters from the army, and thieves of every deſcription continually join theſe people, who reſide in the midſt of foreſts impenetrable to regular troops, where they have little communities of their own, and are governed by chiefs whoſe daring actions and ſuperior villainy have rendered them worthy the honour of ſupreme com-

command. We were alarmed in the dead of night by repeated meſſages from the zemindar of a village about ten miles diſtant from our cantonments, entreating our immediate aſſiſtance againſt a numerous body of Collories, who had ſurpriſed the defenceleſs inhabitants, and ſet fire to their huts after ſtripping them of every thing that was worth the trouble of taking away. This news, however unpleaſant the circumſtance muſt have been to the poor frightened villagers, was highly agreeable to us, as we had long wiſhed for an opportunity of chaſtiſing theſe robbers, who had even deceived the vigilance of our centries, and more than once availed themſelves of the darkneſs of the nights to ſteal the horſes of the Indian officers, which were picketed at the ſkirts of the cantonments. Two hundred of our men were mounted with the utmoſt haſte, and the management of this expedition given to me, not a little proud, I aſſure you, of being ſo ſoon entruſted with ſuch a weighty command. I marched

with

with as much diſpatch as the darkneſs and the uneven road would permit, and arrived juſt at the break of day on the ſcene of action, where the enemy, little expecting our approach, were careleſsly packing up their plunder, and were going off in ſcattered parties, perfectly ſatisfied with the ſucceſs of their enterpriſe. Our ſudden arrival threw them into the greateſt conſternation, the major part immediately ſeeking their ſafety in flight, and ſome few whom, deſpair had rendered valiant, diſcharging their matchlocks and ruſhing among us with their pikes and ſabres. However, this unequal conteſt was ſoon decided, about ſeven and twenty of the moſt daring lying dead upon the ſpot, and near twice that number having proſtrated themſelves on the ground and begged for quarter, which I had no little difficulty in perſuading the enraged ſeapoys to grant them, even the Indian officers having killed and wounded ſeveral who on their knees implored their lives. The loſs we have ſuſtained on this occaſion is incon-

inconſiderable, only one ſeapoy being killed, and a jemadar and three horſes ſeverely wounded. The country people, who had now returned to the village, aſſiſted us in ſecuring our priſoners, who were confined under a ſufficient guard within the walls of a pagoda, while we procured ſome refreſhment for ourſelves and horſes. The zemindar, whoſe inner apartments had been rummaged, and even his women ſtripped of their bracelets and other ornaments, overwhelmed me with civilities, and covered my ſhoulders with a beautiful ſhawl. I ſpent the remaining part of the day with him, and the following morning conducted my priſoners to Wariapollum, a little fort garriſoned by the nabob's ſeapoys, and built on purpoſe to check the inroads of this banditti. Here I ſaw upwards of a hundred of the ſame gentry who had been taken at different times, and had ſuffered the amputation of the right foot and left hand, as an example to their brethren, and to deprive them of the power of com-

mitting

mitting farther miſchief. Twelve of my priſoners immediately underwent the ſame operation, and were condemned to perpetual impriſonment, loaded with chains of an enormous weight, and allowed juſt a ſufficiency of rice and water to preſerve their lives, and to prolong their miſery.

I ſpent two days at Wariapollum, the commandant of which is a German highly in favour with the nabob, and has been a ſoldier of fortune from his cradle. Taking an evening walk with him through the village which ſurrounds the fort, I ſaw a moſt ſhocking inſtance of the fatal effects which are produced by the bite of a ſnake. A man in cultivating his little garden trod upon one of the moſt venomous ſpecies, called by the Indians the covery capelle, and known to travellers by the name of the hooded ſerpent. The creature bit him in the leg a little above the ankle, and in leſs than half an hour the unfortunate wretch expired in the greateſt agonies. The natives, who are groſsly deficient in medical ſkill, know of no remedy againſt the poiſon of a ſnake. The venom of a ſcorpion or centipede is removed by the application of the ſnake-ſtone, which after it has abſorbed the poiſon drops off immediately, and if put into water or milk hiſſes for ſeveral minutes, and turns the latter as green as graſs. Whether it is a compoſition or a natural ſtone I could never learn. It is ſold for a few pence by every itinerant mountebank, and is certainly a moſt valuable acquiſition. The ſnakes are numerous throughout India, and ſome of them of an enormous ſize. It is almoſt incredible to what a degree of obedience the ſhowmen bring them, who teach them to dance and to play a thouſand antic tricks, and handle them with the utmoſt familiarity. The covery capelle at the word of command rears itſelf up, ſpreads out the hood with which its head is covered, and ſeems perfectly to underſtand every nod and motion of its maſter.

I left Warriapollum ſufficiently impreſſed with ſentiments of abhorrence and dread

dread for the whole race of ſnakes, and marched my detachment back to Chillingbrum, where I received the congratulations of my commanding officer. I aſſure you, Alexander the Great, when he paſſed the Granicus, could not have been prouder of his victory, and I ſhall date the æra of all my military glory from this event.

LETTER XV.

Chillingbrum, Nov. 1775.

I Have had the pleasure (if pleasure can be derived from such an awful scene) of being eye-witness to the ceremony of a Gentoo lady burning herself on the funeral pile of her husband. As these voluntary martyrdoms but seldom happen, the crowd collected on the occasion was so very great as to cover the major part of an extensive plain, in the centre of which the lady was to go through this fiery trial into the joys of paradise. I had some difficulty to make my way through the multitude, but as an Indian mob is not quite so uncivil as that which sometimes assembles in the streets of London, I at last accomplished my purpose, and as I sat on my horse within a few yards of the pile, I had a full and uninterrupted view of every circumſtance that paſſed. On the top of this pile, which was of conſiderable magnitude, and built in form of a pyramid, the corpſe was extended under an alcove of withered branches, and adorned with garlands of flowers. At the head and feet were ſeveral pots of burning incenſe, and over the breaſt was ſpread an elegant ſhawl covered with hieroglyphic figures. I had waited about half an hour, when the ſound of the trumpets announced that the proceſſion was began, and the people retiring on each ſide made way for the unhappy victim, who was to be offered up a ſelf-devoted ſacrifice to a barbarous ſuperſtition. She appeared to be in the bloom of youth and beauty, and her form was elegance itſelf. She walked ſlowly with a majeſtic pace, and her countenance betrayed not the leaſt ſymptom of uneaſineſs; but I obſerved a wildneſs in her eyes, which I afterwards learnt was the effect of opium and other intoxicating medicines, which

from

from the moment of the husband's death had been forced upon her by the priests, to dispel her natural fears, and inspire her with a degree of artificial courage sufficient to support her throughout this awful ceremony. When she approached the pile I could plainly perceive her colour change, and had not the priests supported her, she would have sunk upon the ground. They however seemed insensible to her distress, and hastily stripping her of the jewels with which she was covered in great profusion they assisted her to mount the pile, and placing her close to the body of her husband they prayed over her till the torches had been applied to the wood below, and the clouds of smoke began to surround them. They then quitted her with so much precipitation that they tumbled into the arms of their brethren below, and in a few minutes, the pile which was hollow in the middle sinking in, the living and the dead together disappeared from our view. Whether she suffered instant suf-

 focation,

focation, or was for any length of time fenfible of pain, I could not judge; for the fky refounded with the noife of ten thoufand inftruments, and with the horrid fcreams of the priefts, who are careful to prevent the cries of the expiring victim from reaching the ears of the deluded multitude.

Thus ended this melancholy fcene, and I returned home fully convinced that no religion can be acceptable in the eyes of the fupreme being, which authorizes the infliction of fuch infernal cruelties even on the meaneft of his creatures. It is a received opinion, that this barbarous inftitution originally took its rife from the frequent inftances of women poifoning their hufbands, and that the wifdom of the legiflature adopted this fatal ceremony as an infallible fecurity againft fuch crimes in future. But I believe it may with greater propriety be attributed to the avarice of the priefts, who perfuade the credulous Indian that the term of purgation is by this means confiderably fhortſhortened, and whoſe profits from the ſpoils of the unhappy victim are in proportion to the rank and opulence of the family to which her huſband belonged.

The Brahmins or prieſts of the Gentoo religion, derive their name from their great founder Brahma, and their laws are written in the ſancrit or ſacred language, known only to the moſt learned of their caſt. They intermarry with no other caſt, and are conſidered by the inferior ranks of people as partaking of a divine origin. They entertain the ſtricteſt notions of female reputation, and the ſlighteſt ſtain upon the honour of a woman is wiped away by her immediate death. But they are not all of the order of prieſthood; the vaikeels or writers who ſettle the accounts of our regiments are of the Brahmin tribe, and they are even employed as ſecretaries of ſtate at many of the Eaſtern courts. Thus much I have already learnt of them, that their virtues are at beſt but negative, while their vices are diſgraceful to human nature, and in the higheſt degree injurious to community. They are temperate, patient of inſults, regular in their lives, and ſtrictly obſervant of their religious ceremonies. But they are deceitful, crafty, and fond of gain. They conceal the moſt unbounded avarice under the pompous ſolemnity of inſpired wiſdom, and like the venerable impoſtors of the Popiſh church they permit their diſciples to rob each other with impunity, while the credulous wretches bring them a ſhare of the plunder to purchaſe forgiveneſs for the paſt offence and indulgence to ſin again. The pagodas ſo numerous throughout India, are, like the rich livings to the prieſts in England, ſo many ſinecures to the Brahmins, and every choultry, or open caravanſera built by the charitable Gentoos on the ſides of roads for the accommodation of paſſengers, is a little eſtate to ſome lazy Brahmin, who levies contributions on the ſuperſtitious and the ignorant.

LETTER XVI.

Chillingbrum, Dec. 1775.

AN accident has happened which has entirely destroyed the unanimity of our corps, and furnished matter of conversation for every English tea-table in the Carnatic. Captain Fitzwilliams, who has lately been promoted to the command of our regiment, brought with him from England a most beautiful lady, whom he had delivered from one of those enchanted castles where unhappy damsels are imprisoned in King's-place, on condition of her rewarding his gallantry with the exclusive possession of her charms. The lovely Maria for some time continued a pattern of constancy, and doubtless would have remained so still, had she not omitted the necessary precaution of bribing to silence a domestic, who in the dead of night, when the pale moon alone shone

con-

conſcious of the theft, ſurpriſed Lieutenant Villars in the very act of entering her bed chamber through a private door that opened into the garden. This unlucky ſpy had long ſuſpected that Maria was unfaithful, and his ſole reaſon for being ſo watchful over his maſter's honour was the hopes of a large reward, which he moſt ſagaciouſly judged would be the immediate price of his ſecrecy. Finding himſelf diſappointed in his views (as the incautious lovers flattered themſelves that fear of the conſequences would prevent a menial ſervant from making ſuch a diſcovery to his maſter) he fled the very next day to Cuddalore, where Fitzwilliams was on a viſit, and imparted to him the dreadful news. The Captain rewarded the man for his intelligence, and arriving at the borders of the cantonment at the break of day, the firſt object which preſented itſelf to his view was the inconſtant fair-one and her gallant taking the air in a cabriolet, and the arm of the lady moſt lovingly encircling the

the waiſt of Villars. You may imagine to yourſelf the Captain's rage, and the confuſion of the guilty pair. Maria was confined to her chamber, and the gentlemen exchanged a brace of piſtols, which fortunately did no other miſchief than grazing the ſhoulder of the lieutenant. This however did not ſatisfy the enraged Fitzwilliams; he loaded Villars with reproaches of perfidy and ingratitude, and drawing his ſword ruſhed with ſuch rage and fury, and ſo little judgment on his antagoniſt, that he received the point of his weapon in his body, and dropped upon the ground. He was immediately carried to his quarters, and the ſurgeon pronouncing the wound to be mortal, I ordered Villars under an arreſt, and took on myſelf the command of the regiment.

The Ameer Ul Omrah being at Cumbaconum, a few miles only from the Coleroon, in the kingdom of Tanjour, I diſpatched an expreſs to him with the fatal news, and began to conſider of paying

ing the laſt honours to my unfortunate commander. My intelligence however proved to be premature, and the ſurgeon to be miſtaken in his aſſertion; for his patient had only fainted through loſs of blood, and the ſword having miſſed the vital parts, a fever was the only danger to be apprehended. My expreſs returned the following day from Cumbaconum, aſſuring me of the approbation of the Ameer in the moſt flattering terms; and Captain Fitzwilliams applied for leave to return to Cuddalore, till his health ſhall be re-eſtabliſhed. Maria is to reviſit Europe, where ſhe will ſoon fall into the hands of ſome other enchantreſs. Her gay ſeducer is to quit the regiment, and I ſhall take the earlieſt opportunity of paying my duty in perſon to the Ameer, and of ſeeing the once populous kingdom of Tanjour.

LETTER XVII.

Chillingbrum, Jan. 1776.

I Have paid my intended viſit to the Ameer, and have been honoured with a moſt gracious reception. He enquired minutely into every particular of the duel, at which he expreſſed great diſpleaſure, and obſerved that it was the duty of a ſoldier to devote his life to the ſervice of his prince, and not wantonly to hazard it in an inglorious combat.

The city of Cumbaconum is of conſiderable extent, and is ſituate in a delightful country. It is rendered peculiarly pleaſant even in the hotteſt ſeaſon of the year by the number of tanks, or artificial pieces of water, which have been ſunk at a vaſt expence in the ſquares and principal avenues, and are ſhaded by rows of trees producing a flower ſomewhat reſembling the tulip, and of an agreeable ſmell.

ſmell. The palace contains numerous ſuits of apartments, halls of audience, and domeſtic offices, and in the centre is a private garden for the ladies of the ſeraglio. The Rajahs of Tanjour formerly uſed this city as a place of retirement from the buſtle of public buſineſs, and here gave themſelves up to the uninterrupted enjoyment of eaſe and luxury. The Ameer had with him a ſplendid retinue of palanquins, and led horſes, and was attended by four troops of dragoons, and a compleat battalion of ſeapoys. Every choultry in the neighbourhood was filled with men and baggage, and every ſtreet in the town with tents. The oſtenſible cauſe of this viſit to Cumbaconum was a deſire to ſee the country which the army of his father had ſubdued, and to conciliate the affections of the people by honouring the different towns with the preſence of their royal conqueror. But he was ſtrongly ſuſpected of other motives, and the Nabob grew alarmed leſt he ſhould take poſſeſſion of the

the fort of Tanjour, and draw over to his interest the troops, who in consequence of their long arrears of pay not being discharged had already shewn a spirit of mutiny, and would have easily been persuaded to join the standard of the rebellious son against his father and his king. However on this occasion he acted with a becoming spirit, and recalling the Ameer to Madrass at once relieved himself from his anxiety, and disappointed the ambitious views of this aspiring prince. The country round Cumbaconum is in higher cultivation, and far more populous than any other part of the Nabob's dominions which I have yet seen. But I am told that the inhabitants daily emigrate to milder governments, and that above three hundred villages have been entirely deserted since the capture of Tanjour. Such is the wretched policy of the East, where the victorious monarch marks his footsteps with rapine and desolation, and disdains to learn that the riches of his kingdom consist not in the splendor of his armies, but in the number and happineſs of his induſtrious and peaceful ſubjects.

If we examine thoſe faithful records of antiquity the writings of the Old Teſtament, it will appear that there is the moſt perfect analogy between the preſent and ancient cuſtoms of the Eaſt. Many of the religious ceremonies, the plurality of wives, and the ſtrict attention to cleanlineſs of perſon ſo accurately deſcribed in the Bible, ſeem to have been handed down without the leaſt variation to the preſent hour. Whenever I ſee an Indian damſel bathing her beauteous limbs in a tank, the adventures of the pious David recur to my memory; but I hope I ſhall profit by his example, and not venture ſuch dangerous lengths after forbidden fruit, as that holy man is ſuppoſed to have gone after the lovely Hittite.

LETTER XVIII.

Chillingbrum, February, 1776.

A Change of government has happened, which has totally overthrown the late ſyſtem of politicks in the Carnatic, and which I fear will render my future proſpects in the ſervice of the Nabob very precarious and uncertain. The arrival of Lord Pigot to ſucceed Mr. Wynche in the government of Madraſs, and the return of General Smith to Europe in conſequence of the appointment of a new Commander in Chief are events equally unexpected and unpleaſing. The merits of theſe gentlemen may poſſibly be very great, and I doubt not but they will fill their reſpective ſtations with honour to themſelves and ſatisfaction to thoſe *wiſe Directors* who have ſent them out; but the univerſal benevolence and affability of Mr. Wynche will long be impreſſed on the grateful hearts of the inhabitants of Madraſs, and the memory of General Smith will ever be revered in India, while either heroic bravery in the field, or the moſt unbounded generoſity in private life ſhall be deemed a virtue. To do juſtice to the character of this gentleman exceeds my abilities. With the moſt conſummate knowledge of the art of war he poſſeſſes all that coolneſs and intrepidity in the day of battle, which alone can conſtitute the accompliſhed General; and when ſurrounded with all the honours of victory, he has ever uſed his power with a moderation which alleviated the diſtreſſes of the vanquiſhed.

Lord Pigot is inveſted with full authority from the Directors to reſtore the kingdom of Tanjour to the depoſed Rajah, and has ordered the Nabob to withdraw his troops from the different forts and encampments in that country.

His

His Lordſhip intends viſiting Tanjour in perſon that he may be preſent at the reſtoration, and the European troop of cavalry is to eſcort him. The Nabob has in vain remonſtrated, and equally uſeleſs have been the repreſentations of the principal gentlemen of Madraſs, who had advanced immenſe ſums to the Nabob on the ſecurity of his Tanjour dominions, and received mortgages on the produce of the enſuing crops. The governor is inexorable, and the princes of the Eaſt muſt ſubmit to that *honourable united company of merchants*, who have decreed that the rights of mankind ſhall be ſubverted, and that the hereditary monarchs of India ſhall quit or reaſſume their thrones at their caprice and pleaſure. We have read of the unexampled acts of cruelty by which the followers of Pizarro deſolated the fertile provinces of ſouth America. We have wept the untimely fate of a once happy Inca, dragged from the ſplended throne of his anceſtors to an ignominious death; and even children have been taught to lisp the melancholy tale of the unfortunate Montezuma. But the nations of the western world have not been the only victims to European avarice. Even the sons of England, who are free as the air they breathe, whose birthright is glorious independance, *and whose monarchs dare not but hold sacred their chartered rights*, blushed not to see the walls of Tanjour stained with the blood of its inhabitants; nor does a British governor, when he restores to a conquered Rajah those dominions, the reduction of which enriched his predecessors, drop a single tear as he passes through deserted villages and once fruitful fields.

LETTER XIX.

Madrafs, May, 1776.

A VERY unexpected fummons has obliged me to pay a hafty vifit to Madrafs, in confequence of the orders fent to every officer bearing the Company's commiffion to quit the fervice of the Nabob of Arcot and join his refpective regiment without delay. On this occafion I have not hefitated to prefer the prefent emoluments which I derive from the Nabob, however precarious they may be, to the fcanty allowance on which the Company fo generoufly permits its fubalterns to exift. I wifh this was the fevereft misfortune that I have now reafon to lament. I have fuftained a lofs which requires all my philofophy to fupport, and the death of Mr. Hancock has deprived me of a fincere friend and generous benefactor. I believe no man ever lived

lived more generally beloved, or died more univerſally regretted. He was the patron of the widow and the fatherleſs, and I pay but a juſt tribute to his memory, when I ſay that in unaffected charity and real integrity of heart he was not inferior to Mr. Haſtings.

Lord Pigot has viſited Tanjour, and put the Rajah in full poſſeſſion of his dominions. The Nabob's troops have left the country, and thoſe of the Company have ſupplied their places to protect the Rajah from future inſults, and to convince him what infinite advantages that prince muſt derive, who is ſo fortunate as to obtain the protection of the Engliſh.

Numberleſs and unavailing are the complaints againſt broken treaties and violated rights. The gentlemen of Madraſs, whoſe fortunes are involved in the general wreck, inveigh in the ſevereſt terms againſt their honourable maſters. The troops deſtitute of the common neceſſaries of life demand their pay from the Nabob, who declares that the violent

deprivation

deprivation of thoſe dominions, which were his by the right of conqueſt and by the law of nations, renders him incapable either to ſatisfy his creditors, or to relieve the diſtreſſes of his faithful army.

The principal agent of the Nabob at Tanjour, whoſe long and approved ſervices had gained him the unbounded confidence of his maſter, was in the fort when Lord Pigot arrived. This man, who is of the higheſt caſt of the Gentoos, deſcended from an ancient and honourable family, and poſſeſſed of a princely fortune, received his Lordſhip's poſitive orders to quit the garriſon at a moment's warning, and even the indulgence of a few hours to arrange his domeſtic affairs and bid adieu to his friends was peremptorily denied him. The Gentoo, with a ſpirit ſeldom to be found among that puſillanimous race, remonſtrated againſt the cruelty of ſuch treatment, and enquired by what authority the Governor of Madraſs preſumed to juſtify ſuch tyrannical proceedings. His reply was reported to

Lord

Lord Pigot, and a ſcene was exhibited to the view of the aſtoniſhed Indians, unexampled in the annals of English tyranny. A party of ſoldiers forcibly dragged him from the inmoſt receſſes of the palace, and the miniſter of the Nabob of Arcot, the repreſentative of a ſovereign whom the Britiſh empire has not diſdained to acknowledge an ally, underwent the diſgrace of a cruel puniſhment from the hands of a common drummer. He is of courſe rejected by his own caſt as infamous, and nothing leſs than a pilgrimage to every pagoda in the Carnatic, and the diſtribution of his whole fortune in offerings to the prieſts can purchaſe the reſtoration of his forfeited honour.

LET-

LETTER XX.

Madrafs, July, 1776.

EVERY thing is now in the greateft confufion at the Durbar. The creditors of the Nabob daily infult him in his palace, and fome thoufands of his army have lately paid him a vifit equally unwelcome and unexpected. He in vain endeavoured to pacify them with promifes, and begged them to return to their duty. The men rendered defperate by diftrefs obftinately perfifted in their demands, and even threatened him with the moft fatal confequences, if he perfifted in refufing juftice to thofe troops, who had fhed their blood in his fervice. This was not a time for the Nabob to trifle. He paid off their arrears, and immediately difbanded them as a punifhment for that mutiny, to which the want of the common neceffaries of life had driven

driven them. The greateſt part of them have entered into the ſervice of Hyder Ally, and thus is the Carnatic left defenceleſs, and the army of his declared enemy is recruited with thoſe men who have formerly fought the Nabob's battles with ſucceſs, and the loſs of whom, ſhould that enterprizing prince again invade his dominions, he will have too much reaſon to regret.

For my own part, I ſhall ſoon reſign my commiſſion, and reviſit Europe. I have received a letter from my father, who in the moſt affectionate terms ſolicits my return, and with great pleaſantry congratulates me on the marriage of Miſs Rivers, and on my fortunate eſcape from thoſe chains, which if once put on the grave alone can remove.

The principal obſtacle to my leaving Madraſs is the want of money. Our regiment has received no pay for this year paſt; and a ſum is now due to me more than adequate to every expence which can attend the voyage. My whole time is taken up in fruitless visits to the Durbar, where a dissatisfied group of creditors daily meet. No sooner has the sun risen, than every avenue to the palace is filled with palanquins and carriages, and in the evening the same faces and the same surly looks are to be seen again. The Nabob receives every body with politeness, apologizes for his want of punctuality, which he attributes to the loss of Tanjour, and repeats the hacknied tale of the cruel treatment, which he has received at the hands of Lord Pigot.

The governor is now at variance with most of the gentlemen of the council. He has forbidden their future visits to the Nabob without his express permission, and two of them, who have dared to disobey these orders, he has suspended from their rank and employments.

How long a government so divided against itself can stand, time only must determine. Whatever may be the event, I shall soon take leave of a place, where the pleasures of society are totally lost in the turbulence of faction, and where thoſe families, who were ſo lately united by the bands of friendſhip, now hourly meditate each others ruin.

On my firſt arrival in India, I confeſs that I entertained very different ideas of a country, where nature had thrown ſo few obſtacles in the way of happineſs. I was charmed with the novelty of the ſcenes which preſented themſelves to my view, and a ſuperficial enquiry gave me no reaſon to change my ſentiments. But I am now become familiarized to acts of cruelty and oppreſſion, and I deteſt a country, over which the glorious ſun of liberty has never diffuſed his genial influence, and where the inſatiate thirſt of gain has ſpread like a contagion through all ranks of men, from the proud monarch of the imperial race of Tamerlane, to the petty tyrant who preſides over an humble village.

LETTER XXI.

Madrafs, Sept. 1776.

A Revolution of a moft extraordinary nature has taken place, and Lord Pigot is now a prifoner. How far the gentlemen, who have ufurped the government of Madrafs, can hereafter juftify their proceedings, I will not pretend to determine; but they have certainly difplayed equal judgment in the attempt, and courage in the execution of their fcheme. I have before mentioned the difagreements which had happened in the council, and the little inclination which the difaffected members had fhewn to fubmit to thofe regulations, which they confidered as arbitrary and unjuft.

The fudden removal of two gentlemen from the fhare which they held in the government, and the confequent ruin in which they faw their fortunes involved, had now blown the latent ſparks of rebellion into a flame, and had united them in one general conſpiracy to revenge their wrongs, and to recover that authority, which they conceived ſo injuriouſly wreſted from them. A plan was concerted to ſeize the perſons of the governor and of his adherents, and it was conducted with ſo much ſecrecy, that till the hour of its actually taking place, Lord Pigot entertained not the leaſt ſuſpicion of what was intended. His Lordſhip uſually ſlept at the garden-houſe, and had come at an early hour into the fort for the tranſaction of public buſineſs. Every thing went on in the accuſtomed channel, and the governor ſeemed to congratulate himſelf on a ſecurity, which the apparent ſupineneſs and inactivity of his opponents did not a little juſtify. Colonel Stuart, commander in chief of the Company's forces, and the ſuppoſed leader of the diſaffected party appeared to have given up his own political principles, and to be ſo perfectly reconciled to the new ſyſtem of government,

ment, that his Lordſhip embraced him as a convert to his opinions, and conſidered himſelf happy in the acquiſition of ſo valuable a friend. The buſineſs of the day being concluded, the Colonel was invited to return in the governor's carriage to the garden-houſe, and it was determined that the moſt unreſerved intimacy ſhould in future ſubſiſt between them. Little did Lord Pigot think that he was at that moment the dupe of the moſt artful diſſimulation, and that a modern Iſcariot was ſo ſoon to betray his maſter with a kiſs. They had ſcarce advanced a quarter of a mile from the fort, when a party of ſeapoys ruſhing from behind the trees arreſted the carriage, and a poſt chaiſe and four at the ſame inſtant drawing up, the Colonel violently thruſt his Lordſhip into it, and the body-guards of the Nabob ſurrounding him, he had the mortification of ſeeing himſelf in one ſhort moment reduced from almoſt regal ſplendor to the loſs of power, of liberty, and perhaps of life. He is now a prisoner in the house of one of the confederacy at St. Thomas's Mount, distant about three leagues from Fort St. George, where he is guarded by a whole regiment of artillery, while the victorious party has assumed the reins of government, and the plyant herd of sycophants, who so lately cringed at his Lordship's feet, now with equal assiduity pay their adoration to the rising sun.

You may imagine the exultation of the Nabob, and the universal triumph of the successful confederates. He makes no secret of the share which he has had in this memorable event, and even publickly boasts of the influence which he now possesses in the council.

Innumerable dispatches are prepared for the court of directors, and every idle man, who wants an excuse to revisit Europe, now solicits to be the messenger of this important news. A frigate is under orders to sail for the red sea, whence an *ambassador extraordinary* is to proceed over the isthmus of Suez, and in less

than

than three months I ſuppoſe every news paper in England will be filled with various accounts of this tranſaction, all equally contradictory to each other and equally devoid of truth.

LETTER XXII.

Madraſs, Jan. 1777.

I Have been long taught to conſider human nature as a medley of imperfection and inconſiſtency, and to believe that the moſt ſenſible men, when under the influence of paſſion, are often liable to the groſſeſt errors. How far I am juſtified in my opinion the following anecdote will in ſome meaſure ſhew.

One of thoſe adventurers who annually emigrate from England, under an aſſumed appearance, and by forged letters of recommendation had procured a commiſſion in the ſervice of the Nabob, and by his ſervility and little cringing arts had lately been promoted to the rank of aid du camp to the Ameer Ul Omrah. He had derived conſiderable advantage from

the

the accidental circumſtance of meeting Colonel Maeleane at the Cape of Good Hope, who had been ſo far impoſed on by his plauſibility as to give him a line of introduction to Madraſs, and had mentioned him as an unfortunate gentleman, who had borne a commiſſion in the Britiſh army, and had run through the ample inheritance of his anceſtors by his extravagance. For ſeveral months this man conducted himſelf with the greateſt caution, and though his manners evidently betrayed the want of a genteel education, and of that natural politeneſs which alone can conſtitute the gentleman, yet as he was inoffenſive in his behaviour, he paſſed unnoticed among the common herd, and his character eſcaped that particular ſcrutiny, which would neceſſarily have been the conſequence of a more elevated ſtation. However our adventurer aſpired to higher honours, and nothing leſs than the command of a regiment of horſe would ſatisfy his ambition, and he meditated the

ſevereſt

ſevereſt revenge againſt the Nabob for daring to refuſe him what he ſo modeſtly requeſted. The impriſonment of Lord Pigot, and the decided part which the Nabob had taken in that tranſaction ſeemed to afford him an opportunity of gratifying his own reſentment, and of ingratiating himſelf with a party, from whoſe wealth and generoſity he derived the moſt ſanguine hopes of reward.

He ſolicited a private interview with the friends of the depoſed governor, and declared to them that the Ameer Ul Omrah had repeatedly offered him conſiderable ſums of money, if he would aſſaſſinate Lord Pigot, and that he had particularly pointed out a tame tyger as the moſt effectual inſtrument of deſtruction, as his Lordſhip might be induced to alleviate the horrors of his confinement by familiarly playing with this animal, which might eaſily be exchanged in the night for one of a moſt ferocious diſpoſition, and would by devouring his unſuſpecting prey

at

at once relieve the Nabob from his apprehensions, and deprive the unfortunate governor of his life.

Strange and inconſiſtent as this ſtory muſt appear, yet it was greedily liſtened to, and the impoſtor was careſſed by gentlemen, who in their cooler moments would have treated the improbable tale and its inventor with equal contempt.

Numerous affidavits of the whole tranſaction were handed about, and the deep views of this deſigning wretch were not diſcovered, till his prevarications when cloſely examined by diſpaſſionate perſons, and his own confeſſion, when the fumes of wine had got the better of his prudence, at laſt expoſed the perjured traitor to public infamy, and covered his ſupporters with confuſion. However he has reaped this benefit from his treachery, that the Nabob with his diſmiſſion has given him all his arrears of pay, and thoſe gentlemen, whoſe credulity he had ſo groſsly impoſed on, have furniſhed him

with

with a ſum to defray the expences of the voyage, on condition of his immediate return to Europe.

The many extraordinary circumſtances attending this affair have naturally produced a very ſtrict enquiry into the origin and connexions of a man, who could have ingenuity to contrive and impudence to ſupport ſo complicated a ſcene of villainy.

It appears that he was formerly a private ſoldier in the Britiſh ſervice, and that being diſmiſſed the regiment with diſgrace, he had for ſome time acted in the honourable capacity of a bailiff's follower, when coming into the poſſeſſion of a few hundred pounds by the death of his father, who kept an alehouſe in St. Paul's Church Yard, he formed the laudable reſolution of becoming ſuddenly a gentleman, purchaſed an officer's uniform and a cockade, and launching into the wide field of adventure acted the farce

which

which I have juſt deſcribed at the court of the Nabob of Arcot.

Lord Pigot is ſtill a priſoner, and each party waits with equal impatience the reſult of thoſe orders, by which the preſent government is to ſtand or fall.

LETTER XXIII.

Madrafs, May, 1777.

LORD Pigot has paid the debt of nature, and the gentlemen, who fat on the jury to examine into the caufe of his death, have brought in their verdict wilful murder againft every perfon that was acceffary to his confinement. The uneafinefs of mind which his Lordfhip laboured under, and the want of exercife during his imprifonment are the pretences by which they endeavour to juftify fo extraordinary a verdict. Indeed a report has been induftrioufly circulated that his death was occafioned by poifon, and obfcure hints have been artfully thrown out, that the neceffary fteps will immediately be taken to bring the fuppofed affaffins to juftice. But the authors of fuch an improbable ftory are mortified to find themfelves treated with that filent contempt

tempt which they deſerve, and the teſtimony of the phyſicians, whoſe integrity and known abilities are above the reach of cenſure, has ſufficiently proved to the impartial world, that the rumour originated in impotent malevolence. Lord Pigot ſome weeks previous to his death had been removed from the mount to the garden-houſe near Madraſs, where he received every aſſiſtance that the affectionate attention of his neareſt relations, and the art of phyſic could afford. But the hour of his diſſolution was at hand, and his conſtitution enfeebled by the climate, and perhaps ſtill more ſo by the anxiety which continually preyed upon his ſpirits, gradually ſunk under the violence of a fever, which ſeldom ſpares even youthful vigour in theſe burning regions. A melanchbly inſtance of the inſtability of human grandeur, and a leſſon to future governors to uſe their power with lenity and moderation.

Had his Lordſhip taken thoſe ſteps, which his own ſenſe and experience ought to have dictated to him, and rendered himſelf popular with the military, he had never fallen a ſacrifice to a party, which he had exaſperated by ſuch ſevere exertions of his authority, and from whoſe reſentment he had every thing to apprehend. But the officers of the army conſidered him as their enemy and they were ſmarting under the loſs of their batta, which in an unfortunate moment of œconomy he had taken from them. The allowance which is given to the army in the field, and is intended to defray the extraordinary expences incident to a campaign, is called batta, and is about equal to the monthly pay. In times of profound peace half-batta is allowed to the garriſons at a certain diſtance from Madraſs. The whole is calculated at ten thouſand pounds annually, which the Nabob of Arcot by his original contract with the Company is bound to pay; a ſum trifling for an Eaſtern ſovereign to beſtow, but the loſs of which reduced to the utmoſt diſtreſs thoſe unfortunate ſub-

alterns

alterns who had no private resources, and whose circumstances required the most rigid œconomy to support that appearance which their situation in life demanded. The succeeding Governor has prudently restored it, and the Nabob, with that spirit of duplicity which is the true characteristic of an Indian, has declared that he never assented to so cruel and so unpopular a measure.

I have for some weeks past resided at a country retirement in an agreeable village within a short mile of the Durbar. I have a small but convenient cottage, and a garden well stocked with fruit, and I divide the expence of house-keeping with Captain Evance of the Honourable Company's service, a gentleman whose engaging manners and sociable disposition have gained him such universal esteem, that no party of pleasure is ever thought complete without him. Most happily formed by nature either to enjoy life himself or to promote the felicity of others, he wisely prefers ease and tranquility to those splendid miseries which attend on ambition and the pursuit of gain. He sings incomparably, is an inimitable actor, and amidst the rage of contending factions he drinks his convivial glass and laughs at care.

I hope my affairs will soon be arranged so as to enable me to set out for Europe. I shall not be incumbered with a troublesome load of wealth, and I at least can boast that my sleep will not be disturbed by the ghosts of murdered Rajahs.

LETTER XXIV.

Madrass, Sept. 1777.

THE day, the important day is arrived, and the usurped administration is no more. Mr. Whitehill is now Governor of Madrass; Colonel Stewart is superceded; and the discordant members of the council are recalled to Europe. The Nabob is not a little mortified to find his faithful friends so soon removed, but he consoles himself with the hopes that sterling gold will not be less efficacious in Leadenhall-street, than at Madrass. I have at last received my arrears of pay, and am preparing for my journey home. My present intention is to travel by land to Bombay, thence to proceed in a country vessel for the port of Suez, and if I can reach the celebrated city of Grand Cairo in safety, I shall have little difficulty in find-

finding my way to England. I already anticipate the exquiſite pleaſure of landing on my native ſhore, and embracing my long loſt friends. Perhaps too I may find ſome yielding fair one, leſs inconſtant than Miſs Rivers, who may receive a wearied traveller into her arms, and by her ſoft careſſes baniſh the ſad remembrance of all paſt misfortunes.

I am now about to take my leave of a country, which has been deſcribed by ſome travellers as a terreſtrial paradiſe, and by others as a burning deſert deſtitute of every convenience, which can make life agreeable. I muſt confeſs that my preſent opinion of India very little correſponds with thoſe firſt impreſſions, which repreſented every thing to my enchanted view in ſuch delightful colours. The face of the country is indeed uncommonly beautiful; vegetation is ſo rapid, that after a refreſhing ſhower the fruits of the earth ſpontaneouſly ſhoot forth, as if by magic; and the climate

though

though hot to an extreme is far from being ſo inimical, as is generally imagined, to European conſtitutions. But the infernal ſpirit of diſſention perpetually ſtalks abroad, and the joys of ſocial intercourſe, the ties of conſanguinity, and the endearments of private friendſhip are ſwallowed up in the undiſtinguiſhing rage of all-deſtructive faction.

The manners of the natives are almoſt univerſally the ſame. The ſtriking characteriſtic of a Gentoo is avarice, and that of a Mahometan is ambition. The former to gratify his darling paſſion will not bluſh to commit the meaneſt frauds, and the latter will not heſitate to attain imperial dignities by the murder of his patron and his king. The religion of a Gentoo muſt ever nip his growing ambition in the bud. The ſon is obliged to follow the profeſſion of his father, nor can all the riches of the Eaſt procure his advancement to a ſuperior caſt. But the meaneſt Mahometan in the army may riſe

to

to the diſtinguiſhed rank of general, and Hyder Ally, than whom a more powerful monarch does not reign in Aſia, was once in the humble ſtation of a private ſea-poy.

LETTER XXV.

Bombay, Feb. 1778.

AFTER a journey in which for three tedious months I have experienced more fatigue than pleaſure, I have reached the iſland of Bombay, and have taken my paſſage on board an Indiaman for Europe. I am already ſo heartily tired of my expedition by land, that I have even perſuaded myſelf to think a cabbin almoſt a convenient habitation, and I have determined to baniſh the recollection of my former ſhipwreck and captivity.

In the beginning of October I took my leave of Madraſs, and proceeded alone to Pondicherry, where the captain of a French veſſel then under orders to ſail was ſo very preſſing in his invitation to me to embark with him, and was ſo laviſh of his encomiums on his ſhip, that I was

was induced to accompany him on board, and to be an eye witneſs of his accommodations. I was not a little entertained with the appearance of a veſſel, which had been deſcribed to me as ſo uncommonly ſuperb. The apartment which he kindly deſigned for me, was a narrow cupboard in the ſteerage, inacceſſible either to light or air; the great cabbin from the dirt with which it was covered ſeemed occaſionally to have been inhabited either by the captain or his pigs; and the crew appeared to be half dead with diſeaſe and famine. I did not heſitate to bid adieu to this ſcene of naſtineſs, and moſt chearfully ſet out with Capt. George Jennings, whoſe intentions were ſimilar to my own, and with whom I had for many years paſt the pleaſure of being acquainted.

Our firſt ſtage was to Trichinopoly, a fort of conſiderable extent and ſtrength, garriſoned by the troops of the Company, where we were politely entertained by Mr. Thomas Underwood of poetical memory,

mory, and formerly of Peter-houſe College, Cambridge.

Here is the greateſt natural curioſity that India affords; a ſolid perpendicular rock of a moſt ſtupendous height riſing in the centre of the fort, and hiding its head among the clouds. On the top is a pagoda, whence thoſe perſons who are not afraid to purchaſe a delightful proſpect at the hazard of their necks, enjoy a diſtinct view of Tanjour though at the diſtance of above twenty miles. The rock is inhabited by innumerable monkies, who are treated by the Brahmins with the utmoſt tenderneſs, and are continually fed by them with rice and fruits. The brute creation is certainly under infinite obligations to Pythagoras, who has thus kindly provided for their ſupport, and whoſe doctrines, though in the higheſt degree abſurd and childiſh, yet are ſo far meritorious as they inſpire univerſal benevolence.

From Trichinopoly we travelled thro' the plains of Mellore, and arrived at the fort of Madura, famous for having held out two obſtinate ſieges againſt the combined forces of the Nabob and Company, in the ſecond of which it was taken by the treachery of a French officer, and the governor, a Mahometan of royal extraction, whoſe gallant defence againſt a ſuperior army deſerved a milder fate, was ſacrificed to the reſentment of the Nabob. From a more generous enemy he would have experienced that mercy, which his grey hairs, his high deſcent, and above all his heroic bravery ſo juſtly claimed. But ſuch is the ſavage policy of the Eaſt, that death and captivity go hand in hand, and the moſt ſolemn promiſes of life and forgiveneſs to the conquered are no longer deemed ſacred by the conqueror, than while the life of the unfortunate priſoner may be conducive to the intereſts of the victorious tyrant.

At Madura we ſpent three days with the commander of the garriſon, and then proceeded to Palamcotta, the moſt southerly fort of any conſequence in the Nabob's

domi-

dominions. Here we were detained a fortnight, till the Rajah of Trevencore had given us permiſſion to travel through his territories to Anjango, when we took our leave of the Carnatic, and entered the coaſt of Malabar through a paſs fortified both by art and nature in the ſtrongeſt manner. The kingdom of Trevencore is ſituate in ſeventy-ſix degrees of eaſt longitude and eight of latitude, diſtant about ſix hundred miles from fort St. George, and bordering on cape Comorin, which divides the Coromandel coaſt from that of Malabar. Here inſtead of deſerted villages and uncultivated tracts of land, we were charmed with the proſpect of a rich and populous country, whoſe inhabitants enjoy thoſe bleſſings which are the happy conſequences of a mild and eaſy government. Very different were thoſe views which daily occurred to us for the preceding month in our dreary journey through the Carnatic. There indeed for a very few miles round the principal forts the villages were populous, and agriculture ſeemed to flouriſh. But all the intervening ſpace was one vaſt melancholy deſert; the fields being forſaken by the farmers, and the villages by the induſtrious weavers, who are by far the moſt valuable ſubjects of the empire, and to whom princes more politic have afforded that protection, which under the oppreſſive government of the Nabob they have long deſpaired of finding.

As ſtrangers are never ſuffered to viſit the interior parts of Trevencore, our guides conducted us through a country interſperſed with woods and lawns by the neareſt roads to the ſea-ſhore, which is covered with innumerable huts of fiſhermen, whom the Portugueſe miſſionaries have converted to chriſtianity. Infinite pains are taken by theſe prieſts to propagate the goſpel in India, and they boaſt of their great ſucceſs in perſuading the unenlightened Pagans to embrace the divine truths of the Chriſtian revelation. But in my opinion their proſelytes do them but little honour, as they conſiſt entirely

of

of the loweſt and moſt deſpicable caſt of people, there being hardly a ſingle inſtance of their prevailing on a Mahometan or a Gentoo to renounce the religion of his forefathers.

The fourth day after we entered the paſs of Trevencore, we arrived at Anjango, a ſmall ſettlement dependent on the preſidency of Bombay, where we diſcharged our palanquin-bearers, and all unneceſſary attendants, and proceeded in an open boat to Cochin, a Dutch town moſt pleaſantly ſituate on the banks of a navigable river, and thence we embarked in a country veſſel for the harbour of Callicutt.

Callicutt, which is now an inconſiderable village, was formerly a magnificent city, and the reſidence of a powerful prince. According to the tradition of the natives it was overwhelmed near two hundred years ago by a ſudden riſing of the ſea, and all its inhabitants periſhed. We anchored on the ſpot where the ancient city ſtood, and as we went on ſhore at low water, the foundations of the buildings were diſcernible to the naked eye. Here the Company have a ſmall factory, which ſupplies Bombay with betel and cocoa nuts, and a gentleman from that preſidency conſtantly reſides. Hyder Ally is at preſent the ſovereign of Callicutt, and his revenue officers at our landing examined our baggage with as much inſolence and brutal incivility, as if they had received the rudiments of their education at Deal or Dover. Indeed an immenſe tract of country extending along the Malabar coaſt is Hyder's by the right of conqueſt, that ambitious prince ſeldom miſſing any favourable opportunity of making free with the poſſeſſions of his neighbours. The natives in this part of India are afflicted with an incurable diſorder, called the Cochin leg, which obliges them to drag on a wretched exiſtence without even the hopes of relief. The limb ſwells by degrees to an enormous ſize, and the body is proportionably emaciated, till the friendly hand of death puts a period to

a ſcene

a ſcene of miſery, which is rendered doubly ſhocking by the tedious progreſs of the diſeaſe. The Indians attribute it, as they do every other complaint, to ſome peculiar quality in the water.

We next ſpent a few days at Tillicherry, a fort belonging to the Company of no great extent, but ſufficiently ſtrong to repel the attacks of an Aſiatic army, and on the firſt of January we came to an anchor in the port of Goa, where the Portugueſe have now only a ſhadow of that power which they formerly poſſeſſed in India. The city of Goa was once famous for the grandeur of its buildings, and the magnificent decorations of its churches, but it is now deſerted and in ruins; a melancholy inſtance how capable bigotry is of ſubverting the moſt flouriſhing governments, and a moſt ſtriking proof, that even war and peſtilence are curſes leſs terrible to mankind, than prieſtcraft and ſuperſtition. Here until very lately the authority of the inquiſition was exerciſed with a ſeverity ſhocking-

ing

ing to human nature, and highly disgraceful to the religion, which it was intended to promote. Not only the Portuguese themselves smarted under the rigour of this tribunal, but even the innocent natives often suffered the most cruel deaths for daring to prefer the religion of their forefathers to doctrines, which it was impossible for them to comprehend, and which from the methods taken to inculcate them must have appeared to the unhappy wretches as truly diabolical.

We spent two days in visiting the convents, and the few elegant buildings that yet remain in this city, which was once the grand emporium of the Eastern world, and on the seventh we passed the harbour and fort of Gheria, which was formerly the residence of the famous Angria, and is still a retreat for pirates, who plunder every defenceless vessel, that is so imprudent as to approach their coasts.

On the fourteenth we reached Bombay, where I have taken up my quarters in a most excellent tavern, till the Indiaman which

which is to convey me home ſhall ſail. Captain Jennings has already engaged his paſſage in a ſloop for Suez, and by him you will receive this packet, and my father will have the earlieſt intelligence of my return to Europe.

The iſland of Bombay is ſituate in ſeventy two degrees of eaſt longitude, and eighteen of latitude, and is about ſeven leagues in circumference. It originally belonged to the crown of Portugal, but in the year one thouſand ſix hundred and ſixty three it was given to Charles the Second as part of the portion of the Infanta Catherine, and that monarch preſented it as a mark of royal favour to the Eaſt India Company, who fortified it at a vaſt expence, and it is now in the elegance of its buildings very little inferior to Madraſs.

The manners as well of the Engliſh as of the natives are much the ſame here as in other parts of India. At preſent the ſettlement not being divided by factions, there

there is more ſociety than at Madraſs, and the ſources of wealth being fewer, there is leſs of luxury and parade than at Calcutta.

I have dined with the governor who is a gentleman of plain good ſenſe and unaffected politeneſs, and has ſat in the chair with equal honour to himſelf and ſatisfaction to thoſe under him for five and twenty years. I have had the pleaſure of ſeeing the beauties of Bombay at the monthly ball, and I have ſpent an agreeable evening with Mr. Draper, who is ſenior member of the council, and is the huſband of the charming Eliza, whoſe fame will ever live in the celebrated writings of the immortal Sterne.

I have now viſited the three great Preſidencies of India, and I aſſure you that I ſhall bid an eternal adieu to the Aſiatic ſhore without the leaſt regret. My utmoſt ambition will in future be to live ſequeſtered from the buſy ſcenes of the gay and unthinking world, and if I can but find an affec-

affectionate partner with whom I may divide my pleasures and my cares, I shall not envy the pride, pomp, and grandeur of the luxurious monarchs of the East.

LETTER XXVI.

London, October, 1778.

MY dear friend's congratulatory letter on my ſafe return has given me the ſincereſt pleaſure, and has not a little added to the joy I felt at finding myſelf reſtored to the embrace of an affectionate parent, and to my native ſhore.

The voyage from India was neither uncommonly tedious, nor attended with any of thoſe unpleaſant circumſtances, which have before occurred to me. We arrived the latter end of April at the Cape of Good Hope, where I again lodged with my old friend the Dutchman whom I have formerly mentioned, and on the twentieth of May we made the Iſland of St. Helena, which at a diſtance reſembles a caſtle built in the middle of the ſea. This iſland is about twenty miles in circumference, and conſiſts of

ſeveral

ſeveral ſtupendous rocks, with intermediate vallies which are covered with a profuſion of herbage, and produce a very great variety of fruits and vegetables. The inhabitants are almoſt all natives of the iſland, and ſeem to poſſeſs an equal ſhare of affability and ignorance. So totally are they unacquainted with any thing beyond the circle of their own little world, that a young lady, at whoſe father's I ſpent an evening, ſeriouſly aſked me if London was not a charming place when the Indiamen arrived in the Thames, and I had great difficulty to perſuade her, that the gaiety of the metropolis of England did not depend upon the arrival of an Eaſt India fleet.

From St. Helena we ſailed under the convoy of a fifty gun ſhip, and on the eighth of Auguſt were releaſed from our floating priſons, and landed on the Britiſh ſhore. At Portſmouth we heard the firſt news of hoſtilities being commenced, and we thought ourſelves fortunate in escaping the grand fleet of France, which it was Mr. Keppel's intention to have chastised so handsomely, had they waited for him till the succeeding morning.

I have now given you a faithful account of my adventures during an absence of near five years from my native country. But the important event, which is to close the scene, is yet to come. You know the intentions of my father, and you have seen the young lady, on whom my future happiness is to depend. I have been introduced in form, and I flatter myself there is no obstacle to our immediate union. You have often told me that matrimonial felicity is by no means connected with that violent passion, which teaches the lover to deify the object of his affections, and renders him deaf to the voice of reason. I subscribe to the justice of your opinion, but I confess that I am at this moment most heartily in love. The harmony of my Isabella's features, and the engaging sweetness of her looks captivated me at once, and her good

sense

ſenſe has increaſed the prepoſſeſſion, which was inſpired by her firſt appearance.

I have now a new ſcene before me. I think that the brightneſs of the preſent proſpect more than compenſates for every paſt uneaſineſs, and I hope that the chequered adventures of my former life have not diſqualified me for the peaceful enjoyment of true domeſtic felicity

I am, &c.

FINIS.